ECOACTIVIST TESTAMENT

EcoActivist Testament

*Explorations of Faith and Nature
for Fellow Travelers*

H. PAUL SANTMIRE

CASCADE *Books* · Eugene, Oregon

Cascade Books
An Imprint of Wipf and Stock Publishers
199 W. 8th Ave., Suite 3
Eugene, OR 97401

www.wipfandstock.com

PAPERBACK ISBN: 978-1-6667-3688-5
HARDCOVER ISBN: 978-1-6667-9572-1
EBOOK ISBN: 978-1-6667-9573-8

Cataloguing-in-Publication data:

Names: Santmire, H. Paul, author.

Title: Ecoactivist testament : explorations of faith and nature for fellow travelers
/ H. Paul Santmire.

Description: Eugene, OR: Cascade Books, 2022.

Identifiers: ISBN: 978-1-6667-3688-5 (paperback). | ISBN: 978-1-6667-9572-1
(hardcover). | ISBN: 978-1-6667-9573-8 (ebook).

Subjects: LSCH: | Nature—Religious aspects—Christianity. | Ecotheology. | Hu-
man ecology—Religious aspects—Christianity. | Creation. | Francis of Assisi,
Saint, 1182–1226.

Classification: BT695.5 S25 2022 (print). | BT695.5 (ebook).

To Laurel

"For God so loved the cosmos...."

—JOHN 3:16 (AUTHOR'S TR.)

Contents

Preface

Since I am now in my mideighties and since, for that reason, I cannot readily anticipate working on yet another book, I want to bring my long, down-to-earth ecoactivist vocation full circle by dedicating this book to the one to whom I dedicated my first volume, *Brother Earth*, more than fifty years ago: the love of my life, my dear spouse, Laurel. Along the way, she has inspired and delighted me by her bright mind, her intellectual integrity, her passion for social justice, her earnest dedication to her flute, her love for her perennial garden next to our home-away-from-home in southwestern Maine, her tenacious commitments to our family, her beautifully intense personal loyalty, her elegant cuisine, her constant companionship, her relentless affirmation of my passion for theology, and her commitment always to fight fair. I am deeply grateful. That I will mention her often in the ensuing pages will therefore come as no surprise.

I am grateful in a different, but still heartfelt way, for New England artist Eric Aho's permission to allow me to reproduce an image of one of his powerful oil-on-linen paintings, *Road* (2018), as the cover of this book. For me, beyond its compelling beauty, this painting illuminates the profound ambiguity that many people of faith confront these days. On the one hand, Aho's painting could be encountered as a kind of judgment-by-contrast of human life today on planet Earth. Seen from this angle of vision, the painting appears to me to be a silent but heart-wrenching lament for the forests of our planet now going up in flames, and for the road to destruction that has been wrought on our lovely green planet by our fixation on the automobile and on the gross consumption of fossil fuels. On the other hand, and this is the interpretation that I prefer, Aho's *Road* can be read as implicit testimony to the biblical promise for both the greater world of nature and for human fulfilment in nature—signaled by what I take to be the majestic figures of the grand trees and by the road itself, images that suggest to me the biblical promise of a highway in the wilderness on the way to the new heavens and the new earth, when all things will be made new.

H. Paul Santmire
Watertown, Massachusetts
Feast of Saint Francis of Assisi, October 4, 2021

1

Prologue
A Testament for Ecoactivists

Give yourself a break. I want to invite you at the outset to do that, as a fellow traveler: as one ecoactivist writing this testament for others. A young Christian who was urgently committed to nature and to justice once said to me, "The world's going to hell in a handbasket, and I barely have time to deal with my to-do list." Give yourself a break, I say. And, as you do, let me help you think once again about God's engaged love for the whole world—for "the cosmos," according to the maxim behind this book (from John 3:16)—and how this kind of self-conscious faith can more deeply undergird your own ecoactivist vocation.

And as you make ready to come along, don't feel isolated. On the contrary, count yourself as a participant in a huge spiritual ecosystem of like-minded souls in the US alone. Countless thousands of people of faith like yourself are already at work and at prayer for the sake of the earth and the poor of the earth, especially through a variety of grassroots faith networks. You may not know about all of them:

- the Disciples of Christ Green Chalice ministry
- EarthBeat, a project of the *National Catholic Reporter*

1

- Presbyterians for Earth Care
- the Episcopal Ecological Network
- the Evangelical Environmental Network
- Lutherans Restoring Creation
- the United Methodist Church Global Ministries EarthKeepers
- Quaker Earthcare Witness
- ecoactivist groups at many church colleges, seminaries, and universities
- green teams working for climate justice in many hundreds of parishes in the US, across the denominational spectrum
- church camps in the US, many of whose programs focus on ecological engagement from faith perspectives,
- Catholic monastic communities committed to responding to the challenge posed to them by Pope Francis's encyclical *Laudato Si'*

As a person of faith who's an ecoactivist, you are by no means alone.

Nor are your felt needs to deepen your own faith unusual. I have rarely met a Christian ecoactivist who wouldn't have been elated to find a way to reflect more intensely on the riches of biblical and theological teachings about God and nature and justice for all creatures. That's the conversation I want to have with you in this book. At the very end, as a matter of fact, I will invite you to "do nothing" for a spell, precisely because you are already tempted to try to do everything and to do it sooner rather than later. For now, I just want to commend you for taking the time to hold this book in your hands. Let me tell you a little about it, by way of introduction.

I

This is my testament. As a Christian ecoactivist myself, I have a story I want to share with fellow travelers. I have been on a faith-journey with nature for more than fifty years, and I want to tell you about some of the things I have learned along the way—autobiographically, biblically, theologically, and spiritually—in personal faith explorations that I hope will encourage you.

More particularly, this is a conversational book, as you will probably already have noticed. It's not a book that constructs a single argument. Rather, I invite you to imagine us talking together about a variety of topics of interest to you and to others like you, one after the other. Consider this book, then, to be the kind of discussion that happens following the guest lecture at your college or at your church conference or diocesan or synodical meeting, when a group gathers around a table with the guest lecturer in some nearby tea house or other drinking establishment. In such a setting, once the discussion gets going, the topics will jump around, as it were. Participants will feel free to speak up whenever a thought or a question dawns on them. No public formalities here.

Your use of this book, moreover, can be flexible. Although I have arranged the chapters in a way that makes sense to me, you can read them in any order. I will also spare you footnotes and a bibliography, so that you can get going and move on with some dispatch. And the book is small enough to allow you easily to tuck it into your backpack or your briefcase so that you can access it on the subway or on a park bench or when you're grabbing a cup of coffee at the corner and waiting for your ride home—whenever you have a few moments for some discretionary reading. Should you choose to access this book online at any time during your day, so much the better.

II.

What theological themes will you meet in the following explorations? Some, I imagine, will be familiar to you, above all the witness of what is perhaps the most quoted passage from the Bible (my own confirmation text when I was thirteen years old), John 3:16, which, as I have already noted, is the maxim of this book. I have translated it literally: "For God so loved *the cosmos* . . ." This book is about God loving *all* creatures—*everykind*, not just humankind, and certainly not just mankind.

Yes, I want to affirm *the old, old story* of our salvation, bequeathed to us in the Scriptures and, in their aftermath, in the church's historic interpretations of that old, old story. But along the way I also want to emphatically affirm *the whole, whole story* of God's purposes with the vast world of nature as well as with the many particularities of human history on planet Earth.

You may also be familiar with some of the controversies I will highlight in this book, such as when I take issue with theological anthropocentrism (human centeredness). But I hope that such discussions, even though you may have participated in them before, will nevertheless prompt you to start thinking with a renewed sense of theological promise.

Other explorations in this book may be totally new to you. Have you, for example, ever thought much about nature praising God? I hope that such thoughts, if they are indeed new to you, or even if they're not, will both excite you and challenge you to modify or to expand your own thinking.

As you may already have surmised, moreover, the following explorations will follow a winding path. Some chapters will present themselves as autobiographical episodes, as they also address critically important reflective issues in ecojustice theology. Others will lead you to encounter historical themes, such as my discussion of Saint Francis. Still others will be first-person spiritual narratives written under the influence of writers such as Henry David Thoreau and John Muir, yet informed at once, I believe, by a deep, biblically inspired faith in the God of the Bible, who loves the whole cosmos. The book will end, as I have already indicated, with a targeted exhortation for ecoactivists like yourself: to consider what it might mean for you to do nothing for a change.

But whatever the topic, whatever the controversy, whatever the narrative, everything in the following chapters has this purpose: to offer biblical, theological, and spiritual support to ecoactivists like yourself, who are now at the front lines of Christian discipleship in this era of planetary emergency.

III.

Then regarding the personal setting of this book: *EcoActivist Testament* hearkens back to a similar little book I wrote over three decades ago. In 1985, as a young white male pastor and aspiring theologian, I joined an interracial church delegation of men and women from the US for a monthlong pilgrimage to southern Africa. This happened at the height of the horrendous apartheid crisis. Our purpose then was to visit Black congregations in South Africa and Namibia in order to learn about their struggles, their vision, and their joys; to offer them as much support as we possibly could; and then to tell their stories when we got home. That trip was a harrowing experience for me. But I came away from it inspired and energized. I narrated that experience publicly in my short memoir, *South African Testament* (1987).

I have a similar kind of personal story to tell in *EcoActivist Testament*. But the crisis behind this little book is global, not focused on one area of the world, and my own encounter with the challenges I have had to face on the ground has unfolded for more than five decades, not just for a month. In South Africa, I witnessed so-called Hippos (armed personnel carriers) rolling ominously at high speeds through the streets of Soweto, and I watched scores of pedestrians hectically scatter. That journey was charged with dramatic issues of life and death, practically every day.

In stark contrast, my vocational life in my own homeland over the last fifty years has been rather uneventful by most standards—until, to be sure, the recent emergence of the COVID-19 pandemic. Still, drama or no drama at home, as I have already indicated, I feel called upon by the God who loves the whole cosmos, toward the end of what has turned out to be a long spiritual pilgrimage of my own, to address the threats of the global ecojustice crisis one last time. For this particular purpose: to support and to encourage Christian ecoactivists like you, who are already involved in local struggles, and who are passionately committed to work to save the whole planet, wherever that calling might take you.

You will soon discover, moreover, if you have not already noticed, that I am indeed engaging in these conversations with enthusiasm. And I mean that word in its root sense—*en theos*, "in God." My intention here is to have a spirited conversation with you—in the Spirit of God, I hope—every step of the way. This hearkens back to my experience in southern Africa.

What most impressed me when I was in Namibia and South Africa was not mainly the sufferings of the majority of the people, which were enormous and wrenching; it was the joy for the freedom struggle that animated so many lives. And much of that enthusiasm, I quickly learned, was predicated on the identification of large numbers with the life of the church, in a variety of its communal expressions. The church was, for a significant segment of those committed to the anti-apartheid struggle, the beating heart of their resistance to the tyrannical established order, and the heart of their fervent hope for a better world. I was especially moved by the power of the songs of those communities of faith and by the poignancy of the hope that those songs carried with them.

My experience back home has been much the same, notwithstanding all the cultural and political differences. The church's worship in the US has deeply moved me over the course of a lifetime, above all in the African American congregation in Boston, Massachusetts, Resurrection Lutheran Church, where my wife, Laurel, and I worshiped for many years, but also, in a quite different way, in the deeply flowing liturgies of the Episcopal monastery, the Society of Saint John the Evangelist, in Cambridge, Massachusetts, which have inspired us since we moved to the Boston area after I retired in 2000.

I can't help it. On any given Sunday in worship, I may embarrass my wife not only by singing at the top of my voice but also by stomping my feet now and again, marching in place, just the way I did back in the days of my worship in southern Africa. During the COVID pandemic, perhaps surprisingly, the same hymnic logic has also prevailed for me. I have worried whether our singing in our living room at the top of our voices, as participants in an at-home Sunday Zoom liturgy, might not have reverberated through our wall in a way that could have perplexed our neighbors in the next apartment.

Which leads me to this particular confession that will probably not surprise anyone who has come this far with me. Although like many other worshipers, I do have my own list of favorite hymns of all time, first among equals for me is the Saint Francis hymn, which will set me swinging and swaying and stomping in just about any worship setting—and which might be heard as the marching music for this book. Here's an excerpt:

> All creatures of our God and King,
> Lift up your voice with us and sing: Alleluia!
> O burning sun with golden beam
> And silver moon with softer gleam
> O praise him!
>
> . . . .
>
> Dear mother earth, who day by day
> Unfolds rich blessings on our way,
>
> . . .
>
> Alleluia!
> The fruits and flow'rs that verdant grow,
> Let them his praise abundant show.
> Oh praise him! ...Alleluia!
> (tr. William H. Draper [1855–1933])

In that boisterous spirit, this book, like its predecessor in 1987, is indeed a testament of faith *and* hope.

IV.

This book could also be called a testament of ecological spirituality. Perhaps the most widely celebrated theological voice in this arena today is Pope Francis's, who in his stirring and probing encyclical *Laudato Si'* has championed the importance of an ecological spirituality for all, for Christians especially, in this era of global emergency, as the beautiful prayer with which he concludes that encyclical movingly shows, here quoted in part:

> All-powerful God, you are present in the whole universe and in the smallest of your creatures. You embrace with your tenderness all that exists. Pour out upon us the power of your love, that we may protect life and beauty. Fill us with peace that we may live as brothers and sisters, harming no one. O God of the poor, help us to rescue the abandoned and forgotten of this earth, so precious in your eyes. Bring healing to our lives, that we may protect the world and not prey on it, that we may sow beauty, not pollution and destruction. Touch the hearts of those who look only for gain at the expense of the poor and the earth. Teach us to discover the worth of each thing, to be filled with awe and contemplation, to recognize that we are profoundly united with every creature as we journey towards your infinite light. (paragraph 246)

But how is such an ecological spirituality to be claimed more generally by Christian ecoactivists? In recent years I have become more and more convinced that narratives of personal experience, fragmentary as they typically are, have an important role to play in helping other Christians to develop ecological spiritualities of their own, alongside the more discursive theological studies like some of my own writings (see the list at the end of this book) or authoritative teaching statements such as *Laudato Si'*.

I hope that this testament, then, in addition to everything else, can be read very particularly as a response to the spiritual challenge before us all in these times. Yes, like many works of Christian reflection over the centuries, this book is about "faith seeking understanding." But the particular faith I have in mind lives in the hearts of people at the front lines of the global ecojustice crisis, who are wrestling with what is perhaps the most serious challenge the human species has ever faced. How are *you* to continue to find spiritual strength—and joy!—for the struggle? Stay tuned.

2

Reclaiming a Vocation

Earth Day Fifty in Retrospect

For me, April 22, 2020, was not just the celebration of the first Earth Day fifty years before; it also was a more introspective occasion that prompted me to do some reflection about a long pilgrimage of my own. By the time of that first Earth Day in 1970, it had already become clear to me that I was being given this strange but captivating vocation by God, to live self-consciously with nature as my constant companion, to give voice to that experience theologically, and somehow to commit my life to engaging the uncertain future of the earth and the poor of the earth.

I want to tell you about this vocation, right at the start, in order to encourage you to think about your own calling more deeply: how God has been leading you and how you are coming to understand more fully God's purposes with humanity, especially the disenfranchised, and with the whole world of nature.

Fifty years ago, to be sure, such a vocational self-understanding, had anyone chosen to announce it in so many words, would have been regarded as an untenable paradox for someone like me, even an existential contradiction. For I was no Henry David Thoreau, profoundly acclaiming the elemental life in Walden. Nor was

I some kind of wilderness prophet like John Muir, precariously exploring the mountains of California or fearlessly finding his way across glaciers in Alaska. Surely I was no technically trained expert like Rachel Carson, who, in studies like *Silent Spring*, could make a compelling scientific case that whole systems of nature on planet Earth were in serious trouble, due to human abuse. Theologically and spiritually speaking, to draw the starkest contrast, I was no one who even remotely resembled that great Christian saint who so profoundly lived with nature, Francis of Assisi, whose words from his Canticle of Creatures I so dearly loved to sing.

I was a conventional, privileged male, middle-class child of mid-twentieth-century white American exurbia who had developed a strange kind of passion for nature and also for justice and for theology, of all things. Nevertheless, I believed at that time— and I believed all the more so five decades later when many of us were celebrating the first Earth Day all over again—that I had been called by God to live with nature self-consciously and faithfully and then to report back about that experience. *To live to tell about it!* Early on, that passion took over my life.

I.

It all began publicly with a commitment in the late 1960s to announce the (even then) oncoming ecological crisis and to outline a religious response for anyone who would listen. My first book, *Brother Earth: Nature, God, and Ecology in a Time of Crisis* (1970), heralded what I later discovered would be, for me, an expression of a lifelong vocation, engaging the then impending earth-crisis, theologically as well as personally.

The book began with an analysis of some long-standing American cultural trends and their problematic legacy. Following the eminent Harvard historian Perry Miller, I argued that American society was then suffering from a deep spiritual schizophrenia, the split between Nature and Civilization. Think of the two great American Henrys: Henry Thoreau and Henry Ford. These figures represent the schizophrenia of the American mind between Nature and Civilization. It's critical, I believe, for Christian ecoactivists in the US today to understand this legacy. Church people in the past, and even today, have often been deeply influenced by the worldviews of both figures—consciously or unconsciously, for better or (all too often) for worse.

The party of Nature—represented by Thoreau—has shown disgust for what it has regarded as the unhinged economic machinations of society and for the industrial devastation and pollution of nature that those machinations brought with them. That party has then championed a return to the vitalities and the simplicities and the peace of green spaces and mountain vistas, far away from the pollution and the social problems and the alleged superficialities of the city.

On the other side, the party of Civilization—represented by Ford—has celebrated the progress that technology and industry and development can bring to society, overcoming the ancient curses of disease and hunger and vulnerability to the vicissitudes of nature, all of which, according to this view, make destructive resource extraction and pollution of the earth a price worth paying. Spokespersons for the party of Civilization also were given to criticizing the party of Nature as essentially escapist and therefore as irresponsible. How, they asked in various ways, could the way of Nature put bread on the tables of America's working classes, whose members needed jobs much more than they needed wilderness experiences?

In *Brother Earth*, I argued that biblical faith in God and God's creative and redemptive purposes—God's love for the whole world—offers us a way to hold the positive values of Nature and the positive values of Civilization together and, at the same time, to avoid the negative tendencies of each worldview on its own, thus offering a way to heal that profound American social, political, and cultural schizophrenia.

In a word, if you take your stand with the biblical God of creation and salvation, who affirms both the goodness of nature and the promise of urban justice, you can, in turn, yourself affirm the goodness and the promise of both, avoiding the pitfalls of each when championed just by itself. In historic American terms, claiming a biblical faith in God for yourself allows you then to affirm the promise of both the wilderness and the city and not to get hung up on the cultural deficiencies of either when taken just by itself.

I published *Brother Earth* the same year as the first Earth Day in the US. So many years ago! In those days, mine was one of only a very few voices addressing ecological issues from a faith perspective. I had to struggle even to come up with a title for that book. My first impulse for the title had been *Our Sister, Mother Earth*, drawing on the language of Saint Francis—as I eagerly was coming to adopt that imagery as my own in those days, almost without thinking about it, from the hymnody of the church.

But in that era many American Christians were highly suspicious of anything that sounded like paganism or nature religion. Those were the days, more particularly, when numerous American church leaders were, in the wake of the great Swiss Reformed theologian Karl Barth, zealously opposed to any kind of so-called natural theology or even any kind of sustained attention to the world of nature itself from a theological perspective. Which is undoubtedly why my publisher did not like the Franciscan language I had in mind: *Our Sister, Mother Earth*. Thankfully, I was able to hold my Franciscan ground and insist on the title *Brother Earth*.

On the other hand, American Christians—especially American Protestants!—had never wavered in their adulation of Saint Francis—a curious fact, perhaps. Seen in that context, the Franciscan-sounding title *Brother Earth* was an ecumenical plus, or so I thought at the time. To be sure, I would later come to publicly express some regret for the choice of that particular title for my first book. This is why.

II.

The year 1970 also marked, for me, the beginning of a new kind of vocational adventure, in addition to my concerns with the ecological crisis and the theology of nature. I had just begun my ministry as Wellesley College's first chaplain. Back then, for sure, not only was that institution a women's college, but women ran the show! It was a women's world. I soon realized that if I were to survive, never mind thrive, in *that* world as a male ecotheologian (a new term in those days), I would have to become a thoughtful champion of a new form of Christian theology that was emerging, ecofeminism.

Full of such thoughts, I invited the Boston College theologian Mary Daly, author of the then (to many Christians) notorious book, *Beyond God the Father* (1973), to speak in the chapel at Wellesley. (After privately consulting with me ahead of time, she publicly walked out of that chapel service at the end of her sermon, in order to announce a new exodus from what she thought of then as Christianity's patriarchal captivity.) She would be the first of many feminist preachers whom I would bring to Wellesley. So it would come as no surprise, then: I soon began to teach a course in ecological theology at the College—the first of its kind at that institution—highlighting the works of feminist thinkers like Daly and Rosemary Radford Ruether.

With such theological insights in mind, I came to realize, as I already have noted, that my instincts for a title for my first book probably had been right. *Our Mother, Sister Earth* would have been a perfect title for my own—increasingly feminist—setting. On the other hand, I subsequently realized that I had been on to something, too, with the title that I did end up choosing.

Why was *Brother Earth* a good default choice? I have lately been rereading the stunning 1998 study by Peter Coates, *Nature: Western Attitudes Since Ancient Times*. This book should be required reading for anyone who wants to do any serious writing or teaching about the theology of nature. Nature has been such a malleable construct in Western history! And views of nature have often, if not always, been mirror-images of other deeply seated social or economic or psychological constructions of reality, some of them destructive.

Consider the implications of thinking about nature as a machine. Images matter. Is nature really like a machine? This is why the word *Brother* in the title of my first book was, in retrospect, such an important choice in 1970. It helped me to begin to chart what was then, and still is, I believe, the best biblically informed kind of ecological theology—a theology that broke away from then commonly held mechanistic visions of nature.

I think it will be helpful to dwell a bit more on such issues at this point, since they've been so critical for the development of recent Christian theology and are often still influential in current discussions of theology and ecology in a variety of church settings. Ecoactivists, in particular, will be well served to be acquainted with these issues. In my view, theologically speaking, it all comes down to this question: *How do we think about nature and God?*

This is a schema of how numerous theologians have answered that question in recent decades:

(1) Nature is the Body of God or the Great Mother.

(2) Nature is a fellow creature of humans.

(3) Nature is some kind of a *thing* or mechanism or platform just sitting there, as it were, awaiting human study, manipulation, development, or even exploitation.

Modern Christian theologians have tended to lean toward either end of that spectrum, often shaping their approaches to nature in terms of either a *maternal motif* or a *mechanical motif.* Some of you will have heard how these poles typically are named. If these terms are new to you, try to master them, because they're critical for understanding today's ecotheological discussions:

At the maternal end of the ecotheological spectrum are *pantheism* (the view that God is all, and that all is God) and *panentheism* (the view that the world is *in* God, or that the world is the Body of God) At the mechanical end the ecotheological spectrum is *anthropocentrism* (the view that God and humans are theology's chief interest, and nature is a kind of stage or machine or resource to be cared for or exploited).

But there's also a theological middle way, between those extremes: That's often called *theism.* I have long chosen this middle way. I have consistently believed, informed by what I have argued is a viable reading of the Bible and the theological tradition (which I sketched along the way in my book *The Travail of Nature*), that it is best to understand nature theologically as a *fellow creature*—that is, *fraternally and sororally*: the earth is neither divine nor quasi-divine nor a mere thing, platform, or machine. This middle position celebrates both nature and humanity in their distinctness but keeps them both on the same level (in no sense divine) as beloved creatures of God, the Creator of all.

Hence my choice of the title for my first book, *Brother Earth*, was, in retrospect, at least as much a matter of theological commitment as negotiation with a publisher. In retrospect, as I have noted, I came to realize that *Sister Earth* would have worked very well, too, had that kind of option not been blocked by my publisher.

So let it be, I often thought to myself in ensuing years: brother or sister earth! This, for me, has long been an exciting insight. Call this *a faith vision of nature framed by fraternity and sorority*. In sum: every creature of nature is a brother or a sister to every other creature, we humans included. Then there is this, from the perspective of today's public discourse: It's best, indeed, to draw on emerging gender perceptions. Every creature of nature is (shall we say) a sibling. With the wisdom of hindsight, then, my first book could well have been entitled *Sibling Earth*.

III.

After the publication of *Brother Earth* in 1970, in addition to many other concerns both personal and professional, I devoted myself to ecological theology and ecoactivism with what some friends thought of at the time as a strange fixation. They said among themselves, often in my hearing, "What else does this guy think about?" The theology and the activism surely have been a lifelong passion for me, predicated on an increasingly urgent anxiety. Not for nothing did the theme of crisis appear in the title of *Brother Earth* in 1970 as well as in other works along the way, virtually all of which were written with our earth emergency deeply in mind.

Here is an additional situational fact for your consideration. Looking back, since 1970 I can see that many if not all of my vocational labors have been *parochial*. I've acted and written self-consciously and publicly as a card-carrying Christian and as a Lutheran Christian in particular, who has aspired to be a *public, ecumenical* theologian and activist. I want to be as honest as I can about this particular heritage. There's a saying I like that a community organizer once taught me: Grow where you've been planted. And that is what I have regularly tried to do.

Over the years, too, I have often recommended to other Christian ecoactivists to try to do the same: work with and within your own spiritual community, as much as you possibly can. You are probably better equipped to address your denominational compatriots in terms that they will understand than others who write and speak and organize from more generalized perspectives. On the other hand, of course, you will be well-advised to keep in touch with the variegated contributions of ecotheologians and ecoactivists throughout the whole church, as best you can. I have found that that kind of ecumenical awareness can be enormously enriching.

This is my particular story. I had a hand in shaping major statements on the environment by the Lutheran Church in America (1972) and the Evangelical Lutheran Church in America (1993), and I continue to serve as a consultant for the struggling but visionary grassroots movement, Lutherans Restoring Creation (see *lutheransrestoringcreation.org)*, one of numerous such movements across the ecumenical spectrum in the US that I have already mentioned.

My most recent book, *Celebrating Nature by Faith*, written in the wake of Pope Francis's epochal encyclical *Laudato Si'*, invites you to take one step backward, in order to take two steps forward. The one step backward that I propose in that book is to review and reclaim some of the comprehensive contributions of American Lutherans to ecological theology and ecojustice ethics and praxis over the past fifty years.

In *EcoActivist Testament*, though, I now want to accent another, still more critical ecumenical theme. I wrote *Brother Earth*, more than fifty years ago, in part to respond to the then increasingly popular 1966 claim by the historian Lynn White Jr.

that Christianity as a faith tradition had been, for the most part, ecologically bankrupt (!). I then argued there, and in many other writings as well (especially in *The Travail of Nature*), that White's thesis was an important *half-truth*. Yes, we must be well aware of how much Christianity has been complicit over the centuries in cultural trends that appear to have led to the abuse and the degradation of nature and the poor of the earth.

But that's not the whole story, by any means. Historic Christianity has also championed a second—ecological!—tradition. Among many others, I argued, the Protestant Reformers Martin Luther and John Calvin gave voice to that tradition. Its chief exemplar, I suggested, was the man from Assisi, Saint Francis.

Thankfully, as the global reach of the environmental crisis has become more and more apparent, the (hitherto not widely known) Christian ecotheological tradition that I have long celebrated has, for a wide variety of reasons, begun to *thrive* in many settings, most visibly perhaps in the theology that came to expression in Pope Francis's *Laudato Si'*, but not only there. Reformed theologians such as Jürgen Moltmann, in his book *God in Creation: An Ecological Doctrine of Creation* (1985), and Catholic theologians such as Elizabeth Johnson, especially with her study *Women, Earth, and Creation* (1993), have made major contributions to ecological theology and ethics, beginning already in the last decades of the twentieth century.

By the end of the second decade of our century, indeed, ecological theology and ecojustice ethics and ecological spirituality and ecoactivism have become major themes in Christian circles around the globe. Virtually every Christian communion in the world now has theologians and activists who are engaging the global crisis. I have even entertained the thought that we now have entered the golden age of Christian ecological theology and ecojustice activism.

IV.

Therefore, on April 22, 2020, the fiftieth anniversary of the first Earth Day, I was able to celebrate my long-standing vocation as an ecological thinker and activist rooted in Lutheran traditions, now in the midst of a global ecumenical community of theologians and practitioners and other activists, led by His Holiness Pope Francis—all of whom have been and are committed to the life and the mission of the holy catholic church and, in particular, to its ecological and ecojustice witness in this, our globally apocalyptic era.

But on that day much more than my vocational trajectory was on my mind. As I was reflecting about the previous fifty years, I found myself sheltering at home and deeply troubled within. The crisis of the coronavirus was then upon us all. I kept thinking that that virulent scourge of nature might well be only a single expression of a number of global disasters that could continue to afflict God's good earth and the people of the earth, especially the poor, in the years to come.

3

Celebrating a Role Model

Saint Francis and the Witness of the Bible

In reclaiming my own ecoactivist vocation and encouraging you about yours, I also want to do all that I can to celebrate the venerable witness of that blessed man from Assisi, Saint Francis. Not for nothing did Pope Francis, a champion of the poor and of all the creatures of the earth, take that name as his own. Could it be that all ecumenical roads in these times of wrenching global crisis might converge in Assisi? Could it be, more particularly, that Francis of Assisi could become *your* patron saint, if he isn't so already?

I.

Francis of Assisi is the hero of a thousand causes. Strikingly, the Poverello (the poor one), as he has come to be called, has not only been celebrated by Catholics and by the current pope in particular, he has also been championed by countless American Protestants for decades. As a sign of this, all over the US, statues of Saint Francis are to be found in innumerable private gardens and for sale in many nurseries as well. And paintings and other images of Francis preaching to the birds are widely treasured by US Catholics and Protestants alike. Meanwhile, a broad range of American Christian churches have in recent years taken to celebrating October 4th as the feast day of Saint Francis—most notably perhaps the congregation and staff at the Cathedral of St. John the Divine in New York City: that celebration features a procession of many striking and some rarely seen animals.

Notwithstanding all this attention, however, the historical Francis is an elusive figure. Much of what we know about him comes to us from sources of varying historical value. A few short writings of his own exist, as do biographical testimonials from a number of his followers—some of whom were close to him and others of whom collected his teachings and also stories about him; yet some of their sources are clearly legendary. Still, we know enough about the historical Francis to understand why he sometimes has been thought of as a second Jesus. He was for sure an extraordinary follower of the man from Galilee.

II.

In the midst of all this attention around Saint Francis, how are we best to grasp the meanings of the man for our own times, particularly what has long been thought of as his love for nature? Library shelves everywhere in the US are full of books about Francis. Methods of interpretation of the life and meaning of the Poverello abound. I propose an idiosyncratic approach that may be familiar to you, depending on your church background.

What I propose is to view him through a biblical lens. Let Francis be Francis, yes. But let us see him, not primarily with our own eyes alone, but with our vision as it's focused by biblical insights. That is what I want to do here, working with biblical texts from a fall season of the church year, with biblical texts which have been adopted by numerous churches in the US. We'll begin with the passages appointed for the aforementioned Day of Saint Francis in October.

So think of yourself, perhaps, as a participant in the grand liturgy celebrated the first week in October at the Cathedral of St. John the Divine in New York City, where any combination of these texts might well be read in its liturgy celebrating the life of Saint Francis. Everyone in that huge congregation would then be challenged to make sense of Saint Francis's life in terms of such texts, with the help of whomever happened to be the preacher that day.

Consider this, then, to be an experiment in historical encounter. What can we learn about Francis when we allow a group of what might be thought of as arbitrarily chosen biblical texts to collide with his life? Consider this also an experiment in historical address. How does the figure of this great saint, who would have been shocked to have been called great, address us today when we seek to hear God's Word afresh as we celebrate Francis's life and witness?

To make this interpretive process work, I hasten to add, you will have to resolve right now to engage the appointed texts that I will be exploring. That's why I have printed them out along the way, for your convenience. Yes, your main interest at this point will be Saint Francis. But be disciplined. Even be eager—to encounter God's Word as a way to grasp the meanings of the Poverello for your own life and for the world.

III.

I want to begin by reflecting on selections from the first group of these lectionary texts, thinking of Francis at this point *as a prophet of God.*

> Two men remained in the camp, one named Eldad, and the other named Medad, and the spirit rested on them; they were among those registered, but they had not gone out to the tent, and so they prophesied in the camp. And a young man ran and told Moses, "Eldad and Medad are prophesying in the camp." And Joshua son of Nun, the assistant to Moses, one of his chosen men, said "My lord Moses, stop them!" But Moses said to him, "Are you

jealous for my sake? Would that all the LORD's people were prophets, and that the LORD would put his spirt on them!" And Moses and the elders of Israel returned to the camp. (Numbers 11:26–30)

John said to him, "Teacher, we saw someone else casting out demons in your name, and we tried to stop him, because he was not following us." But Jesus said, "do not stop him; for no one who does a deed of power in my name will be able soon afterward to speak evil of me. Whoever is not against us is for us. For truly I tell you, whoever gives you a cup of water to drink because you bear the name of Christ will by no means lose the reward." (Mark 9:38–41)

Have you ever wondered what the *numbers* are in the book of Numbers? The Hebrew title for this biblical book, perhaps confusing to us, is "In the Wilderness." But *that* reveals the major themes of this biblical book. The English construct Numbers is something else.

This is where the title of this book comes from: It refers to two censuses taken as the people of Israel, having received the law at Mount Sinai from Moses, stand ready to proceed toward the promised land. The book of Numbers basically tells us about the people journeying on from Egypt and about some of their trials and tribulations along the way.

We meet a generational theme, too. Numbers recounts how the first, rebellious generation of the Israelites gives way to a new and more promising community of the faithful. The book ends, then, with that second generation about to enter into the promised land. The final form of Numbers probably was shaped by the Hebrew people's experience of exile in Babylon, long after the events it records but not too long before the people returned to Judah in the Holy Land.

Saint Francis frequently claimed such In-the-Wilderness themes as his own. He was not first and foremost a lover of nature, as he is sometimes portrayed, although he certainly was that. He was first and foremost, self-consciously, a follower of Jesus. Francis exemplified extraordinarily throughout his ministry what Dietrich Bonhoeffer in our own era thought of as "the cost of discipleship." Like Jesus, Francis gave up all his worldly goods so that he, Francis, could become a follower of Jesus. Frequently, too, like Jesus, Francis sought out remote places, akin to what we think of wilderness areas, for prayer and meditation and rest. Indeed, so much did Francis identify with Jesus that the Poverello, toward the end of his life, as he found himself in the wilderness of Mount Laverna, experienced the stigmata, the marks of the crucified Christ, on his own hands, side, and feet. I read this experience as attesting to the power of Francis's faith and his total identification with Jesus. Francis's faith somehow claimed his very body with a huge charge.

But Saint Francis was by no means just a pilgrim in the wilderness. He was all the more so a public preacher. That's why I'm suggesting that we think of him as a *prophet of God*. He took his message of repentance for the many and hope for the forgotten ones of this world, like the lepers, to the city centers of his time. In the era of the Crusades, moreover, when many political and religious leaders—above all, the venerable spiritual leader Saint Bernard of Clairvaux—were marshalling resources and rallying people to *make war* on "the infidels," Francis made a perilous journey of his own around the Mediterranean to visit personally with Sultan al-Malik in Damietta, Egypt. The purpose of that adventure of faith was to be a prophet *for peace*, not for war.

In this respect, Francis was like Eldad and Medad in the book of Numbers, who were prophesying not in the tent of meeting with Moses and all the elders, but all by themselves back in the camp, as our text tells us. Francis did not find his primary place in the courts of power, whether in the hierarchical church or amid those of high economic or political standing, although he was always a loyal son of the Holy Catholic Church.

Francis's witness, in this sense, was a lonely one. He preferred to minister to the lepers outside the walls of the city rather than associate with the urban elite. Francis called upon all Christians of his time, indeed, to become prophets for the sake of the little ones of the earth, who had been excluded from the common good. The words of Moses about Eldad and Medad could easily have been Francis's own: "Would that all the LORD's people were prophets, and that the LORD would put his spirit on them" (Numbers 11:29).

And Francis was controversial, as a matter of course, as most prophets typically have been. In this respect he also was like Eldad and Medad. This is that story: Joshua, Moses's right-hand man, objected to the fact that Eldad and Medad were prophesying back at the camp. Joshua demanded that Moses get those two under control. Likewise, public objections to Francis emerged early in his ministry, in particular when he ventured outside the walls of his own hometown in Italy, Assisi. Francis had decided to be with the lepers and other homeless poor, who had been forced to live under trees or in hovels, vulnerable to the elements and without easy access to food, water, or shelter of the kind that the people who lived inside the town could take for granted much of the time.

As a prophetic figure in this sense, one who prophesied outside the tent of the meeting where the powerful of his time had congregated, Francis was as a matter of course perceived as a threat to the established order, especially when people from all walks of life began to follow his example. He was joined by many followers and cheered by crowds in the cities, too, where people in the streets expectantly listened to him.

But, of course, as I have noted, the established society of his day, like all established societies, did not want things to change, yet change is always a possibility in the wake of such popular movements. Like Joshua in Moses's time, people of social standing in Francis's day were troubled by any kind of freelance public prophesying. They typically did not want any Eldad or Medad raising their voice among the common people, outside the hierarchies of established power.

The story is told of a young American Christian some years ago who went on a mission trip to join a team that was working with some impoverished farmers in Nicaragua. There she encountered living conditions that she had never seen before. There she also realized that her own government had in no small measure helped to hold the then oppressive ruling Nicaraguan regime in power. There, too, she heard talk among the people of the land and their priests about Jesus's mission to liberate the poor. In response, her life was transformed. She came back from her trip and began to tell members of the congregation which had sent her there to join with her in behalf of "the liberation of the oppressed."

But her message was not generally well received. Even her own pastor seemed to shy away from her language. Still, she persisted—and as a result she was marginalized in her own congregation. If only she had had a Moses around, who could have celebrated her prophetic work. If only the people of her congregation, some of whom might well have statues of Saint Francis in their gardens, could have appreciated how thoroughly Franciscan her spirit was!

If only, too, the members of her own congregation and her pastor had deeply understood the Gospel story from Mark 9. There we hear John saying to Jesus, "Teacher, we saw someone casting out demons in your name, and we tried to stop him, because he was not following us." (Mark 9:38) But Jesus replied, "Do not stop him." The young woman's pastor could have said to his congregation, "Do not stop her." And that pastor might have cited the example of Francis, who ministered to the lepers outside the walls and visited the sultan in the name of Jesus and the peace that Jesus embodied.

Francis did everything he did as a follower of Jesus. He took up his own cross in the name of Jesus. He reached out to the poor in the name of Jesus. He preached to the multitudes in the name of Jesus. His own body, indeed, came to be marked, as we have already seen, by wounds like Jesus's. For Francis, Jesus was the Lord of life and death. Francis's celebrated love of nature can only be understood in light of that love for Jesus, the deepest love of his life.

In this sense, the man who preached to the birds was first and foremost a prophet of the God whom Jesus, the prince of peace, had claimed as his own.

IV.

Secondly, consider the following diverse and apparently discon-
nected texts, as we now reflect about Francis as *a child of God*.

Then the LORD God said, "It is not good that the man
should be alone; I will make him a helper as his partner."
So out of the ground the Lord God formed every animal
of the field and every bird of the air, and bought them to
the man to see what he would call them; and whatever
the man called every living creature, that was its name.
The man gave names to all cattle, and to the birds of the
air, and to every animal of the field; but for the man there
was no partner. So the LORD God caused a deep sleep to
fall upon the man, and he slept; then he took one of his
ribs and closed up its place with flesh. And the rib that
the Lord God had taken from the man he made into a
woman and brought her to the man. Then the man said,

"This at last is bone of my bones
	and flesh of my flesh;
this one shall be called Woman,
	for out of the Man this one was taken."

Therefore a man leaves his father and his mother and
clings to his wife, and they become one flesh. And
the man and his wife were both naked, and were not
ashamed. (Genesis 2:18–24)

O LORD, our Sovereign,
	how majestic is your name in all the earth!
You have set your glory above the heavens.
	Out of the mouths of babes and infants
you have founded a bulwark because of your foes,
	to silence the enemy and the avenger.
When I look at your heavens, the work of your fingers,
	the moon and the stars that you have established;
what are human beings that you are mindful of them,
	mortals that you care for them?
Yet you have made them a little lower than God,

and crowned them with glory and honor.
You have given them dominion over the works of your hands;
    you have put all things under their feet,
all sheep and oxen,
    and also the beasts of the field,
the birds of the air, and the fish of the sea,
    whatever passes along the paths of the seas.
O Lord, our Sovereign,
    how majestic is your name in all the earth! (Psalm 8:1–9)

Long ago God spoke to our ancestors in many and various ways by the prophets, but in these last days he has spoken to us by a Son, whom he appointed heir of all things, through whom he also created the worlds. He is the reflection of God's glory and the exact imprint of God's very being and he sustains all things by his powerful word. When he had made purification for sins, he sat down at the right hand of the Majesty on high, having become as much superior to angels as the name he has inherited is more excellent that theirs. (Hebrews 1:1–4)

Some Pharisees came, and to test him they asked, "Is it lawful for a man to divorce his wife?" He answered them, "What did Moses command you?" They said, "Moses allowed a man to write a certificate of dismissal and to divorce her." But Jesus said to them, "Because of your hardness of heart he wrote this commandment for you. But from the beginning of creation, 'God made them male and female.' For this reason a man shall leave his father and mother and be joined to his wife, and the two shall become one flesh."

Then in the house the disciples asked him again about this matter. He said to them, "Whoever divorces his wife and marries another commits adultery against her; and if she divorces her husband and marries another, she commits adultery."

People were bringing little children to him in order that he might touch them; and the disciples spoke sternly to them. But when Jesus saw this, he was indignant and said to them, "Let the little children come to me; do not

stop them; for it is to such as these that the kingdom of
God belongs. Truly I tell you whoever does not receive
the kingdom of God as a little child will never enter it."
And he took them up in his arms, laid his hands on them,
and blessed them. (Mark 10:2–6)

Francis in many ways *was* childlike. He spoke to the birds, as
a playful five-year-old might do. Like many children, too, Francis
also loved to sing. He was said to have joined once with a flock of
birds in their singing. As he lay dying, indeed, Francis kept singing
his now famous Canticle of Creatures over and over again.

Francis also invented the Christmas pageant, which for children in recent decades in our world has become one of the most
beloved of their church experiences. This is how that happened.

Toward the end of his life, one Christmas Eve Francis gathered some farm animals around a makeshift altar in a mountain
woods in Greccio, some sixty miles from Assisi. He also invited
people of all classes of society to join with him and the animals.
There he sponsored a Eucharist outdoors, at which he sang the
Christmas Gospel text. Francis has instructively been called "God's
Troubadour" (before his conversion to the life of poverty, as a rich
young man, Francis had learned to cherish and to sing the songs of
courtly love!). Like a child, Francis loved to sing.

Above all, as Francis's Christ-Mass reminds us (and again like
some children—though not all), Francis famously loved animals,
even worms, even wolves. His preaching to the birds is of course
widely known and celebrated today. Perhaps more than any other
saint that we know, Francis embodied these words of Jesus: "Let
the little children come to me; do not stop them; for it is to such as
these that the kingdom of God belongs" (Mark 10:14).

If Francis was a *prophet of God*, as we have seen, he was all the
more so a *child of God*. He was a child of God par excellence. But
at this point we meet an interpretive puzzle. The theme of childhood isn't always attested unambiguously in the Scriptures. On the
contrary, it would appear that another image is sometimes *more*
prominent in the Bible, or at least that the Bible is sometimes read

that way—the image of *lordship*. God is King and Jesus is Lord, we hear again and again in the church.

Soberingly, then, in keeping with such language, numerous Christians over the centuries have believed—on what they have thought was good biblical grounds—that "the man is the head of the woman." Likewise for this theme, "humans are given dominion over nature." Where does the theme of the child fit into all this talk about human lordship?

Soberingly, too, the texts before us appear to accent the lordship theme in many ways. According to Genesis 2, the man names all the animals, apparently as if he owned them. The woman, made from the man's rib, is brought to the man, as if he's the one who's really in charge. In Psalm 8, we are told that humans are but a little lower than angels and that they are given dominion over the works of God's hands—indeed that all things have been put under human feet: sheep and oxen, even the wild beasts. The Letter to the Hebrews cites this psalm and says that all things are subjected to Jesus. Is there a suggestion here not only that Jesus is Lord, but that he is prone to "lord it over" others?

Then there's lordship and marriage. The Gospel of Mark seems to present us with the (apparent) teaching of Genesis about marriage all over again, although Mark's handling of this theme does suggest a certain equality between the man and the woman, insofar as the state of being divorced is concerned. Still, where is the childlike innocence and the childlike joy and the childlike singing in all this? Marriage here in this Markan context seems to be all about rules and regulations, with one dominating head (the man) calling the shots, rather than about free-flowing love and uplifting joy and deep loyalty between two equal partners.

But no. The Gospel reading *can* be—and, I believe, it *should* be—understood as authorizing a different kind of vision: not in so many words, but more in terms of its juxtaposition of texts. This is the way that I recommend reading it.

Mark seems to string together various teachings by Jesus at this point in his Gospel. On the one hand, there is Jesus's teaching about divorce. On the other hand, there is Jesus's teaching about childlike faith. There's no logical or even narrative connection between the two accounts. They are just strung together. Jesus taught this and Jesus taught that. If so, then these questions follow: Which theme is to be interpreted in terms of the other? Which is more important for the Gospel's sake, human lordship or human childlikeness? Surprisingly perhaps, centuries of Christian interpreters have opted to make lordship the primary image for interpreting the Scriptures, not childlikeness.

But what if Jesus meant what he said when he singled out a child and said that to such as this one belongs the kingdom of God? Aren't children, then, not lords, the point of it all? Further, couldn't this thought possibly open our eyes to a different reading of these biblical texts? Couldn't we call Saint Francis to mind here, too? Think of his childlike simplicity and his innocent reaching out to the little ones of his world. Above all, think of his powerful caring for all God's creatures.

Strikingly, Genesis 2 tells us that "the man gave names" to all the animals. In the past, this has typically been interpreted to mean that the man *lorded it over* the animals. On the contrary, a more careful reading of this text shows that "giving a name" is *an act of love* according to the Old Testament, an act of bonding, even friendship, as when God calls Israel by name. Think of Francis here, too, whose exemplary life as a child of God led to his bonding with animals. In the Hebrew Bible, likewise, when God calls *you* by name that means that God *loves you*. This appears to be the meaning when we hear about Adam naming the animals. Adam, once again, is *bonding* with the animals, not claiming control over them.

Also, why was Adam put in the garden in the first place? To "till it and keep it"? To exercise mastery over the Garden as some kind of lord? That has been the popular reading of Genesis 2:15 until very recently. The Hebrew actually says, however, that the man was put in the Garden to "*serve and protect it.*" And the word "serve" here is from the same family as the word for "Servant of God" in Second Isaiah, a text that was read from the very beginning by Christians as referring to Jesus. Serve and protect—doesn't that sound like Francis relating to the animals of his world? Doesn't that sound like a child caring for a dear and beloved animal, as farm children often have done?

When it comes to the text before us from the book of Hebrews, which is essentially a lordship text ("he sat down at the right hand of the Majesty on high"), we are starkly faced with a fundamental interpretive decision. Is this *the* primary text for interpreting the mission of Jesus, or are we to look to another, say, Philippians 2:5–11, which envisions Jesus Christ primarily as *the Servant of God*? In Philippians 2, "Lord" essentially means the "Servant of all." Why can't this be *the* primary text for our biblical interpretation? Which, indeed, is closer to the heart of New Testament faith for understanding Jesus: being a lord or being a servant?

All of which, I believe, is an invitation to read the Scriptures all the time with the eyes of Saint Francis, that astounding child of God and servant of all.

V.

Lastly, consider these texts, which yield, in my reading, a counter-intuitive theme: Francis was not only a prophet of God and a child of God. These texts show us that the Poverello was, paradoxically, *an heir of wealth*.

> Seek the LORD and live,
>> or he will break out against the house of Joseph like fire,
>> and it will devour Bethel, with no one to quench it.
> Ah, you that turn justice to wormwood,
>> and bring righteousness to the ground!
>
> . . .
>
> Seek good and not evil,
>> that you may live;
> and so the LORD, the God of hosts, will be with you,
>> just as you have said.
> Hate evil and love good,
>> and establish justice in the gate;
> it may be that the LORD, the God of hosts,

will be gracious to the remnant of Joseph.
(Amos 5:6–7, 14–15)

Turn, O Lord! How long?
Have compassion on your servants!
Satisfy us in the morning with your steadfast love,
so that we may rejoice and be glad all our days.
Make us glad as many days as you have afflicted us,
and as many years as we have seen evil.
Let your work be manifest to your servants,
and your glorious power to their children.
Let the favor of the Lord our God be upon us,
and prosper for us the work of our hands.
(Psalm 90:13–17)

Indeed, the word of God is living and active, sharper than any two-edged sword, piercing until it divides soul from spirit, joints from marrow; it is able to judge the thought and intentions of the heart. And before him no creature is hidden, but all are naked and laid bare to the eyes of the one whom we must render an account. Since, then, we have a great high priest who has passed through the heavens, Jesus, the Son of God, let us hold fast to our confession. For we do not have a high priest who is unable to sympathize with our weaknesses, but we have one who in every respect has been tested as we are, yet without sin. Let us therefore approach the throne of grace with boldness, so that we may receive mercy and find grace to help in time of need. (Hebrews 4:12–16)

As he was setting out on a journey, a man ran up and knelt before him, and asked him, "Good Teacher, what must I do to inherit eternal life?" Jesus said to him, "Why do you call me good? No one is good but God alone. You know the commandments: 'You shall not murder; You shall not commit adultery; You shall not steal; You shall not bear false witness; You shall not defraud; Honor your father and mother.'" He said to him, "Teacher, I have kept all these since my youth." Jesus, looking at him, loved him and said, "You lack one thing; go, sell what you own, and give the money to the poor, and you will have treasure in heaven; then come, follow me." When he heard this, he was shocked and went away grieving, for he had many possessions.

Then Jesus looked around and said to his disciples, "How hard it will be for those who have wealth to enter the kingdom of God!" And the disciples were perplexed at these words. But Jesus said to them again, "Children, how hard it is to enter the kingdom of God! It is easier for a camel to go through the eye of a needle than for someone who is rich to enter the kingdom of God." They were greatly astounded and said to one another, "Then who can be saved?" Jesus looked at them and said, "For mortals it is impossible, but not for God; for God all things are possible." (Mark 10:17–27)

Francis grew up the son of a rich cloth merchant. It was assumed that Francis would "sow some wild oats" during his teens, and then settle down into a plush career in his father's business. Instead, as a young man Francis plunged into what we moderns sometimes call "an identity crisis." Early on in his life, he became profoundly troubled by his own riches and his own raucous lifestyle. Francis then became a penitent, as numerous seekers had done in his time, and took to living in the woods or in places like abandoned churches.

In a striking response, Francis's father, for his part, abandoned his son, with intense anger. The father had wanted a son fashioned in the father's own image. Francis would have nothing to do with that. Francis wanted to fashion his image to reflect the example of Jesus.

Things came to a head when the local Bishop, Guido, who had befriended Francis, called Francis and Francis's father, Pietro, to Guido's church, to effect a reconciliation. The father had never, to that point, accepted the fact that his son had rebelled against all that the father had held dear, above all his riches and his social standing. Would, then, the son be reconciled to the father?

No. At that meeting in the church Francis went into a nearby room, took off the elegant clothes that came with his social standing, and came back to reveal the penitent's hair shirt he had been wearing underneath all of them. He then laid his old, elegant garments at his father's feet.

Francis thus renounced his own father, in the name of "Our Father who art in heaven," and began what was to become a life-long ministry as a penitent, as a preacher, as a servant of God's little ones, as a sometimes solitary mystic, as a keeper of all the church's rituals, above all the Eucharist, and as a celebrant of the creatures of nature.

By most standards, then, Francis, this heir of wealth, had made himself poor. By his own standards, Francis believed that he, by abandoning his worldly inheritance, had made himself rich. In this ironic sense, I'm calling him an heir of wealth.

Of what do true riches consist? This was a tough question in Francis's day. It is perhaps even more difficult for many Christians today, particularly for those of us who have benefited so much by living affluently in the US. The texts before us help us to wrestle with this question, especially when read in light of Francis's life-long commitment to what he considered to be the true wealth given to him by God, poverty.

Strikingly, the prophet Amos brings a harsh judgment against those who benefit unjustly from the kind of riches that Francis left behind: "Ah, you that turn justice to wormwood, / and bring righteousness to the ground!" (Amos 5:7); "You who afflict the righteous, who take a bribe, / and push aside the needy at the gate" (Amos 5:12). It's easy to think here of the top 1 percent in the US today and their unjust share of the world's wealth. But from a global perspective, *most* Americans today are among the world's affluent. Is there any hope, then, for any of *us* who are rich by global standards?

For all his damning words, surprisingly, Amos seems to think that there *is* hope for the likes of us. This is what he calls us to do: "Seek good not evil, / that you may live; / and so the LORD, the God of hosts, will be with you" (5:14).

And who is this God of hosts? The God of grace, of course. Thus the psalmist prays: "Let the favor of the Lord our God be upon us; / prosper the work of our hands" (Psalm 90:17). And the writer of the Letter to the Hebrews calls us to approach God's "throne of grace with boldness, so that we may receive mercy and find grace to help in time of need" (4:16). The God attested by the Bible is ready to embrace us all, never mind what our economic status might be.

But there's a complication here—*Jesus*. Surely, Jesus *does* affirm the unconditional grace of God, announced by the psalmist and by Hebrews. But Jesus apparently also wants *more*, as we see in the Markan text before us. A man runs up to Jesus and asks Jesus what the man has to do to inherit eternal life. Jesus checks him out, we can imagine. Is the man eager to change his life? Is the man perchance feeling guilty?

It turns out that this particular man has numbered himself among "the good people," those who keep God's commandments and who follow God's ways, presumably like most worshipers in many American congregations on any given Sunday in our own world. Actually, the man seems to be astounded that anyone would even *ask* him about his own life, how *he* follows the ways of God. He was that sure of himself. He thought of himself, as perhaps you or I think of ourself—as a "good person."

Jesus understood the man instinctively. Indeed, Jesus loved the man, we're told. And this was a great love, on Jesus' part. The Greek word for "love" here, is *agape* (pronounced "ah-gah-pay"), pointing to the self-giving love of God Godself—the same word that appears in what I'm calling the maxim of this book—John 3:16, "For God so *loved* the cosmos . . ." Out of this boundless and overflowing love, Jesus says to the man: "You lack one thing; go, sell what you own, and give the money to the poor, and you will have treasure in heaven; then come, follow me" (Mark 10:21). Is Jesus asking the man to adopt a kind of Franciscan vocation?

The man, we are told, "was shocked and went away grieving, for he had many possessions" (Mark 10:22). One can wonder what preachers in affluent American congregations are inclined to make of this passage—if they will deal with it at all. But never mind those preachers, what can many members of the church in the USA say? What can you say? What can I say?

Soon after this, Jesus says to his disciples, "How hard it will be for those who have wealth to enter the kingdom of God" (Mark 10:23). Like those American preachers and their affluent congregations, we might imagine, the disciples were perplexed. The text has certainly perplexed me.

But Jesus tightens his point even more: "It is easier for a camel to go through the eye of a needle than for someone who is rich to enter the kingdom of God" (Mark 10:25). Like many (most?) affluent American Christians who hear these words, and like many preachers, too (myself included), with the disciples, we throw up our hands! We ask, "Then who can be saved?" (Mark 10:26). Jesus responds with what must be regarded as one of the most frustratingly opaque but ultimately most hopeful pronouncements he ever made: "for God, all things are possible" (Mark 10:27).

All this Grace around us, given for us who are affluent and given with the promise that God will find a way for us to be wealthy toward God and not dependent on the money that we think we need! What are we affluent Christians really to do? Francis wrestled with these questions as a young man, and he abandoned his riches. Francis gave away the wealth of his earthly father in order to claim the wealth of his heavenly Father. Some affluent Christians today will surely think about doing the same. Some have. But what about the rest of us? What are *we* to do?

A couple of commonplaces of worldly wisdom come to mind. This is the first: don't just sit there feeling guilty, do something. Second, a more congenial piece of advice: a journey of a thousand miles begins with a single step. What might that something, that single step, be?

Here both Jesus and Francis can offer some counsel. Both of them focused their ministry on the little ones, on those forgotten by the dominant, wealthy classes. Could we do the same? Francis, more particularly, fleshed out Jesus's concern for the little ones by explicitly including the creatures of nature in his ministry. Francis self-consciously and publicly loved the birds and other animals, with the kind of *agape* love that he had learned from his Lord, Jesus. Could you and I go and do likewise?

Here's one caveat: a close reading of both the lives of Jesus and Francis shows that, for them, the suffering little ones are thus burdened, in some significant measure, because of the powers of *unjust human institutions*, the kind railed against by the prophet Amos. For Amos, it was the banking system (as it were) that caught his attention. For us, it could be our banking system. It could also be global energy companies, such as those that by default, if not by intention, promote climate change. Think, then, of global energy production and the unending quest for profits by the powerful, on the one hand, and of rising ocean waters that threaten to engulf millions of poor people living on low-lying lands in Bangladesh, on the other.

More to the point, did you know that just *one-hundred companies* around the world today are responsible for some *70 percent* of climate pollution? Did you know that Exxon Mobil, most egregiously, knew as early as the 1970s that the way it was doing business would lead the world into the kind of climate crisis we find ourselves in today? Did you know, further, that, in response to such corporate iniquity, a number of church-based action groups, among them numerous Catholic sisters, have been finding ways to join with a variety of public interest groups to pressure companies like Exxon to change their evil ways? Have you ever thought that the Lord might be calling *you* to participate energetically in one of these campaigns? If you have already involved yourself in such protests, have you done that, self-consciously, in the liberating names of Jesus and Saint Francis? If not, why not?

On the other hand, never mind the overwhelming challenge of addressing the global climate crisis today. For now, *just do something.* Take that first—or that next—step. Christian participants in the great climate change march in New York City in the fall of 2014 marched by the thousands. Even affluent Christians who had little to offer but their bodies and their songs (and later, hopefully, more than generous financial support for good ecojustice causes) reported experiencing a palpable joy that day, for them a joy born of the Grace of God, experienced at that moment.

More recently, with a spirit of enthusiastic confidence, many Christians (most of them young people of faith) took to the streets with thousands of others to demand that the nations of world, meeting in Glasgow in 2021, change their meandering and lethargic ways of responding to the global climate crisis and deal it head on and without delay. Those protesters had found a way to take some public steps—with enthusiasm—in behalf of ecological sanity and human integrity around our beleaguered planet. Perhaps that enthusiasm, in some small measure, was the kind of joy that Saint Francis experienced all the time—only for him all the more so, because he had been such a wealthy man at the outset, by worldly standards, and his vocation from God was so clear to him.

What steps does our situation of global injustice and vast environmental havoc mandate for each of us, who, with Francis, seek to be lovers of the poor and lovers of nature? Are *we* ready to embrace the poor and the creatures of nature, in the name of Jesus and inspired by the example of Saint Francis? Does each of us stand ready to take the next steps that the God of Jesus and the God of Francis is calling us to take? If we are to celebrate Francis as our role model, there's no better place to begin than by responding to those questions.

4

Entering A Forest

Spiritual Practices and the Immediacy of God

Recalling that forest near Greccio in Italy now, where Saint Francis once sponsored that, for us, famous Mass on Christmas Eve centuries ago, come with me now to a very different forest setting known only to a few today: come with me to the foothills of southwestern Maine, where, at the edge of Round Mountain, many years ago, I worked now and again, over the course of several summers, to carve out a path, winding up and around at the edges of a steep, boulder-strewn, tree-covered slope.

There's to be no Christ-Mass to witness here, no gathering of animals and people from different classes, to celebrate the birth of the Savior. We see only a lone soul who is seeking, however precariously, to enter into the presence of the same God who so blessed that Christ-Mass of Saint Francis centuries ago. Think of your own forest walks as I tell you this story. What has been revealed to you? What would you still like to know?

I.

I love to enter that forest and to saunter up and around and down that path whenever I can, to let my mind wander, to contemplate the larger things of life, and to encounter surprises along the way: a huge fallen branch from a two-hundred-year-old oak, a pristine rhododendron blossom, the gracious gliding of a pileated woodpecker, the mysterious footprints of a moose. For me, this walk is a way of loving the creatures of nature in the spirit of the Poverello, but mundanely and modestly.

But I couldn't do the walking without the raking. In the fall that path totally disappears underneath a thick covering of oak and beech leaves. When that happens, even I, who know that path well, sometimes have trouble following it along. Still more of a problem, if the path isn't raked, it can be hazardous. Left to itself, that carpet of dry leaves is like a sheet of ice. The leaves cover over fallen branches, too, which can trip you. If that happens, you might easily careen down the path and smash into a tree or even fall over a ledge. Hence my regular raking.

I have only realized in recent years, after the publication of my book *Before Nature: A Christian Spirituality* in 2014, that that raking and that walking help to tell the evolving story of loving nature that I narrate in that book. After many walks in those woods over the years, my understanding of God was challenged, and it changed. My approach to spiritual practices changed as well.

I want to tell part of that story here, because spirituality is all the rage these days, especially the spirituality of nature. But not all the available options feel authentic. What *is* a real, biblically informed spirituality of nature? I know that that question is in all likelihood on your mind. Over the years, I have heard numerous ecoactivists express interest in finding more viable ways to engage nature spiritually.

Sometimes this has taken the form of a desire to learn more about the spirituality of Indigenous peoples in what is now the US, insofar as that's possible. I affirm that kind of spiritual quest as long as it's authentic and doesn't settle for some popularized amalgam of

European and American that is only called indigenous but doesn't truly reflect the lives of Indigenous people. But there's something to be learned, too, from the ancient Greek proverb "a bird in the hand is worth two in the bush." Actually, I've long been excited by a fresh reading of the spirituality of nature available in what have perhaps been too little known or sometimes misunderstood Christian traditions, which are there for the taking, as long as you know where to look for them. I therefore hope that the following reflections, which are rooted in historic Christian traditions, will help you to find a spiritual way that makes sense to you or even that gives you more confidence in following the course that you've already chosen.

II.

I was baptized in 1935, "in the Name of the Father and of the Son and of the Holy Ghost." Years later, beginning in the late 1960s, when, as I have already noted, I served as the chaplain of Wellesley College, I found myself questioning the spirituality that I had inherited with my baptism.

In those days (again, as I've previously observed) I invited feminist theologians to preach in the college chapel where I presided—people such as Mary Daly and Rosemary Radford Ruether. In no way, then, could I escape wrestling with the charge they made that Christianity, with its accent on "God, the Father almighty," was *spiritually destructive*, precisely because it celebrated, or was alleged to celebrate, the rule of a dominating, exploitative male Deity. They also argued that the vision of a domineering heavenly Father led in practice to the domineering exploitation of the earth.

Those feminist theologians were not the only ones in those years who objected to historic Christianity on the grounds of its allegedly destructive approach to nature. Many other critics said the same, often on the basis of historical analysis of the role that the Christian faith—especially the activist Reformed tradition— was said to have played in fomenting modern industrial society's exploitation of nature. Christians, said many of these critics, care only about God and humanity, not about nature. Christians, according to the same critics, regard nature as mainly a very useful source of raw materials to be used for the upbuilding of human society.

Well, no. Many Christians, over the centuries, have loved nature in itself, above all Saint Francis of Assisi, but not only him. Read rightly, the whole Christian tradition carries within it *a major tradition*—notwithstanding other traditions that point in other directions—that has affirmed and even celebrated nature. Not for nothing, therefore, as one who had long aspired to become a student of Christianity's ecological promise, did I carve out and care for and walk along that ascending and descending forest path in southwestern Maine. But what kind of spirituality had led me to desire to create and to walk that path?

III.

Early on in my vocational trajectory, I decided that the critics, overall, had their point. As a lover of nature, who was struggling to be a faithful Christian, I would therefore have to rake away a lot of dead ideas if I were to uncover the viable spirituality of nature that I instinctively knew was there underneath it all. The understanding of *God* that I inherited would have to change, to begin with. Fortunately, others had begun to respond to the same kind of challenge, in their own settings.

First, I learned from the Reformed theologian Jürgen Moltmann how God the Father can helpfully be engaged as God "the motherly Father." Thus understood, according to Moltmann, we also can envision the Father as suffering with the Son on the cross. In a word, God the Father is not some dominating and distant heavenly patriarch, far removed from our distress or the anguish of other creatures.

In my own language, I came to understand that God the Father is the eternal *Giver*, who, as Luther believed, is "in, with, and under" the whole creation. God the Father loves *the world*, as John 3:16, my confirmation text and this book's maxim, says. God the

Father doesn't just love humans. And God the Father, in concert with the Son and the Spirit, will therefore, one day, bring *all things,* not just humans, to fulfilment and joy in the bosom of God, as the book of Revelation's vision of a new heaven and a new earth so vividly illustrates.

Second, I learned that God the Father alone is not the Creator, even though our creeds, understood just by themselves, tend to leave us with that impression. The whole Trinity is the Creator. Thus the Son is the "cosmic Christ." That conviction is attested variously in the New Testament, but especially in the Letter to the Colossians, as the Lutheran theologian Joseph Sittler helped me to understand. According to Colossians, Christ is "before all things, and in him all things hold together."(Col 1:17) The Spirit, likewise, is the "Lifegiver" of all creatures as the Nicene Creed affirms, a thought highlighted most instructively by Elizabeth Johnson. This image is especially vivid in Genesis 1:2, where we see the Spirit hovering creatively over the primeval waters of the world coming into being. If the Father is the Giver, then, as I came to realize, the Son is *the Gift* and the Spirit is *the Giving.* So the whole Trinity is richly and graciously involved throughout the whole history of creation and redemption.

Third, I learned from a range of biblical scholars who had studied ancient Christianity in the context of the Roman Empire that the earliest expressions of the Christian faith in God, the Father of Jesus, were totally opposed to the domination or the exploitation of anything. The God whom Jesus proclaimed, according to the Gospel of Luke, for example, is the God who liberates the poor and who lets the oppressed go free, as we can hear Mother Mary sing in the hymn—to which I will return in Chapter 9—that has traditionally been called the Magnificat (Luke 1:46–55). The God whom Paul announced, as we will see more particularly in Chapter 6, is a God who hears the groaning of the whole creation and who works to liberate the whole creation. As Paul says in Romans 8, "the whole creation has been groaning in travail" (v. 22) and will itself "be set free from its bondage to decay and obtain the glorious liberty of the children of God" (v. 21).

For Paul, more particularly, this God is revealed in the ministry of Jesus Christ. And that ministry is nonviolent and compassionate. For this reason, Paul spiritually distanced himself from the violent and self-exalting lordship of Caesar, including Caesar's destructive policies toward the world of nature in his own day. Scholars have shown that members of the churches in Rome, to whom Paul wrote, would have well understood "the groaning of creation" that Paul talked about in Romans 8 as referring, at least in part, to Roman desecration of the natural world—ravaging the soil in North Africa, for example, in order to keep the city of Rome supplied with grain—in the process of bolstering the empire's own wealth and power.

IV.

With my spiritual path thus cleared of old and questionable ideas and having identified those new understandings of God as one whose power is made known in sacrificial serving—directed even to the least of God's creatures—I also realized that I would have to "walk the talk" of prayer in a new way. I concluded that my long-standing regimen of Sunday worship and daily prayers over meals and in the morning and at the end of the day was not enough. Somehow I would need to develop a deeper awareness of God—Father, Son, and Holy Spirit—in the whole creation every moment of my life. Could I learn to "pray without ceasing," as the Scriptures admonish us to do (1 Thessalonians 5:17)?

Providentially, when I was a graduate student I came upon a Christian tradition that practiced precisely that kind of approach to prayer. A number of Orthodox writers and practitioners had championed what they thought of as "the Jesus Prayer," in order explore what it might mean to pray without ceasing. I began to adopt constant repetition of that prayer as best I could, not without a number of false starts. Then I took it further, as I worked on developing my own spiritual practices.

The prayer I eventually learned to say regularly begins like that Orthodox prayer, by calling on Jesus and asking for his mercy.

In my view, that's the best way for all of us sinners to begin our prayers. But I needed to be more explicit about other equally essential themes of the classical faith of the church. Hence the prayer I began to use regularly goes beyond a plea to Jesus for mercy. It moves on to center on the mystery of the Trinity, the name in which I was baptized and the God whom I had been seeking, for many years, to know in, with, and under the whole creation, as Father, Son, and Holy Spirit.

My prayer then concludes by calling on the Spirit to sanctify all things, to realize all the promises of God for the whole creation and to do so without delay. I call this "the Trinity Prayer":

> Lord Jesus Christ, have mercy on me.
> Praise Father, Son, and Holy Spirit.
> Come Holy Spirit, come and reign.

All these are ancient Christian themes, obviously. That's why, as a matter of fact, they speak to me so powerfully.

I have found that repeating the Trinity Prayer as often as possible during the day—weaving in the new understandings of God as Father, Son, and Holy Spirit that have been given to me since my days at Wellesley College—can work to keep me on a good spiritual path as far as nature is concerned: because the God whom I thus constantly address is the God of the whole creation, who is working everywhere and without ceasing, in manifold and mysterious ways.

I take special delight in repeating that prayer again and again—sometimes even *singing* it to the tune of the Doxology or other hymns—while I walk by myself along that forest path in southwestern Maine. What, I wonder, do the squirrels that are harvesting acorns in that forest feel when they hear such sounds?

V.

I hasten to add that for me, my raking and walking and singing this way in the cathedral of the great outdoors on any given day during the warmer seasons in southwestern Maine, also presupposes my walking into and worshiping within the cathedral of the great indoors, in churches that Laurel and I have frequented in Boston. More than two decades into retirement, I continue to be a devout churchgoer and also an ardent advocate of ministry in the city, notwithstanding all the time Laurel and I spend in rural Maine. In Boston, too, I do everything I can, both publicly and privately, to help those who are struggling to address life-threatening climate-change challenges. But those are stories for another setting.

Here I want to talk about my own spirituality of nature as it has claimed my interiority, toward the end of my life. It's a regular raking and a frequent walking along that forest path, and other places like that, which I hope I can continue to follow as long as I am given the breath of life, praying the Trinity prayer as often as possible, sometimes under my breath, sometimes even singing it, as I have said: thus constantly being aware of the Father, Son, and Holy Spirit as the God of everykind, not just the God of human-kind (as I observed at the outset), and surely not just the God of mankind.

This prayer I recommend as a tested Christian way to inspire love for nature, imitating the love of God for whole world, the cosmos. Here it is, again:

> Lord Jesus, Christ, have mercy on me.
> Praise Father, Son, and Holy Spirit.
> Come Holy Spirit, come and reign!

And along the way, as you keep repeating these words, don't disparage the walking and don't disparage the forest itself. They're not steps up some ladder to some allegedly higher spirituality beyond the forest, say, in the silent solitariness of your own soul as you might think of it, soaring up in your interiority toward heaven. These steps along such a forest path are *already* fully located in God's presence. There's no higher place than that.

I have found those steps to be revelatory, too, in a way that, say, kneeling on the floor in my study and uttering my prayers before the large Latin-carved wooden head of Christ over my desk may not always be—or even that kneeling in a corner of the stone chapel of the Episcopal monastery in Cambridge might not always be. On that winding forest path, I am not quite my own, as I am in my study or in the protected spaces of the monastery sanctuary. As I walk along that winding path, there is no danger of me nodding into spiritually sluggish moments, as I occasionally do when I'm kneeling in my study or even, sometimes, when I'm at prayer in solitude in the monastery chapel.

Indeed, the forest itself has a way of keeping me at the porous edge of things and not closed in upon my own subjectivity. Being completely thrown off guard when you trundle into a flock of quail at first totally invisible to you but then exploding in every direction—that's astounding. Likewise, when you happen upon four—rarely seen—woodcocks silently and slowly processing in formation on the forest floor, like ballet dancers. Such experiences claim your undivided attention. And you wonder: Where is God in all this, and what is God saying to me now?

Or the sight of the familiar stone wall (to any who have ever visited or lived in rural New England) running through the forest. People once tried to farm that rock-strewn land! That's why those walls are there. They had to put the boulders somewhere. And they had to clear those fields by hand and horse. Those walls are signs of those arduous efforts. The human pilgrimage with God on this earth sometimes *is* harsh.

In the forest, one can also know instinctively that God has purposes with the creatures and the contours of the land that may be alien to ours and to our sensibilities and often are. God was there when the glaciers ruled the land, grinding and splintering stones much larger than the ones that were so arduously set into my picturesque New England wall two hundred years ago. Who am I to feel secure in that forest, moreover, however safe I may have kept those paths, when God is working so majestically with so many other creatures of nature, visible and invisible? When the wind rushes through the tops of the trees above, with disquieting sounds, how can I feel at ease within? Awe is what this situation calls for, rather than a feeling of safety or contentment.

If, for example, I stand at the base of a towering white pine, perhaps more than a hundred years old, and if I look up that grand and powerful trunk through the branches toward the bright but refracted light so high above, even feeling some vertigo, as a matter of course I say to myself "My God!—Praise Father, Son, and Holy Spirit! My God!" And I make the sign of the cross. Awesome it is looking up through the branches of that colossal tree into the sometimes-blinding sunlight. The biblical proclamation feels true: no one can see God and live.

VI.

I am helped in sensing all this, spiritually speaking, by my Lutheran theological inheritance. This can sound a bit quirky to people who may be theological newcomers. But hear me out. This particular theological heritage offers spectacles for my soul, so to speak, through which I can the more intensely envision the majesty and the mystery of God with us and near us as I wander up and around and down that swept forest path. I like to tell as many people as I can about this heritage. It's ecumenically enriching, I believe.

To be sure, this heritage brings with it a lot of spiritual baggage, above all the failings of Martin Luther himself. His publicly announced attitudes toward Jews and peasants were reprehensible. Justifiably or not, the Nazis found it all too easy to call on Luther to support their horrid anti-Semitism and their unspeakable Final Solution. But just because some mushrooms are poisonous doesn't mean that, if you have eyes to see, you can't harvest others. However plain this analogy, I find it helpful. It sometimes does take a lot of training and much experience to be able to identify good insights embedded in some of the poisonous traditions of Lutheran theology. But I believe that the effort can be worth it.

I have written at length about Luther's theology of nature, especially in my book *Celebrating Nature by Faith*. Here I only want to give some hints about Luther's theology of God's presence in the world. I invite you to resolve self-consciously to come along now, as I probe some of these complex theological riches. This effort, like the uncertain pace of a guest of mine in Maine some years ago, a newcomer to that forest, walking cautiously behind me along the path that I had raked, will be well worth the effort, I believe. Why, by the way, shouldn't an existential encounter with God be complicated? Who said that all things Divine should be simple or reassuring or understandable!

Martin Luther was influenced by the mystical traditions of Western Christianity, particularly by that tradition's willingness to invoke the discourse of *paradox*—images of faith colliding with each other or even contradicting each other. Luther loved, for example, to quote the traditional mystical saying that "God is the circle whose center is everywhere, but whose circumference is nowhere."

The twentieth-century German American theologian Paul Tillich, who deeply respected the faith intuitions of Luther, once observed that given the fact that we humans inhabit a finite world yet seek to know an infinite God, there's a logical place for paradox. If you, a finite creature, want to speak about an infinite God, in other words, everyday language won't suffice. Finite language must be broken—judiciously to be sure, but broken nevertheless— in order to speak meaningfully about an infinite God. Luther did that.

Luther's preferred way to speak of the presence of an infinite God in the finite world was to invoke many prepositions. So God is not just *in* the world, Luther could say, the way grain is in a sack. As we have already heard Luther say, God is in, with, and under the whole world. Nor would Luther want to hear that the world is *in* God, say, the way a fetus is in a mother. That's just too literal a way of thinking, from Luther's angle of vision.

From Luther's point of view, strange as this might sound, we don't know anything about the relationship of the world to God! It's the other way around. What we *do* know, especially from the Scriptures, according to Luther, is *what God is doing in the world*, although that, too, is shrouded in mystery. Yet what we do know of God's relationship to our world is truly amazing, overwhelming, and astounding, in Luther's perspective.

This is a characteristic utterance of Luther about the nearness of God to nature—what traditional theology calls *the immanence of God*. If you're not familiar with this kind of paradoxical thinking, be patient with yourself and ponder these words slowly, given their spiritual intensity:

> God is substantially present everywhere, in and through all creatures, in all their parts and places, so that the world is full of God and He fills all, but without His being encompassed and surrounded by it. He is at the same time outside and above all creatures . . . [T]he Divine Majesty is so small that it can be substantially present in a grain, on a grain, through a grain, within and without, and that, although it is a single Majesty, it nevertheless is entirely in each grain separately, no matter how immeasurably numerous these grains may be.

When you're walking through the woods, in other words, you don't have to look up to the heavens above to find the ineffable God, although that God is there, surely, the Light of lights. When you're walking in the woods, nor do have to imagine probing spiritually into the incandescent mystical depths of your own soul to find the ineffable God, the Ground of Being, although that God is there, surely, as well. Rather, God is all around you: in every oak tree, with every downy woodpecker, under every granite ledge, with every mosquito, in the thunder that you might hear ominously resounding from the other side of the mountain; yet God is not encompassed by any creature or movement of nature, but rather is majestically absent from the forest around you, even as God is nearer to you than you are to yourself.

Permit me to say still more about this theme, as I take so much delight in celebrating God's presence this way—I don't want to stop. God—Father, Son, and Holy Spirit—mystically permeates that forest and stirs like a whirlpool of energy in, with, and under every boulder and every fern and every American beech and every trampling moose and every bolt of thunderous lightning, as well as with and within the heart of any human creature who might be walking along that forest path. Yet at the same time, according to

Luther's paradoxical way of seeking to grasp these mysteries, even as *God fills all things* (according to one of Luther's favorite biblical passages, Ephesians 4:10), for Luther, *God is also nowhere.*

5

Encountering Treehood

The Faith of an Amateur Arborist

Has anyone ever called you a tree hugger? I have heard that epithet a number of times in public settings when I addressed a variety of audiences, uttered following my talks during the question-and-answer time, in what was alleged to have been jest. Which sometimes had a chilling effect on my soul. But over the years I have learned to take that epithet in stride, even to celebrate it.

Turns out, I *am* a tree hugger. Call me an amateur arborist, in the root sense of the word *amateur*, a *lover* of trees. You will perhaps have concluded as much, having walked with me through the previous chapter. With countless saints and sinners throughout the ages, I have long pondered and celebrated the mysteries of trees. I cannot think too much about trees.

When I was a young graduate student, for example, and I happened to read a popular essay which claimed that the great gothic cathedrals of France, with their soaring arches, originally had been envisioned by architects who themselves had been inspired by the experience of human life in or near the towering and overarching branches of ancient forests, I immediately decided that that insight must be true. Isn't a primeval forest just as sacred as a gothic cathedral? Should we be surprised, therefore, when the one mirrors the other?

When, in my eighties, I visited the Basilica of the Holy Family designed by Antoni Gaudi (1852–1926) in Barcelona, I was sure that those spiritual intuitions of my younger years had not been in vain. I looked at that sacred building, and, astoundingly, I *saw* trees! That whole towering and enveloping modern cathedral-like structure is held in place by stone-sculpted tree-trunk columns. Each of those massive pillars, in turn, supports the church's canopy with curvaceous, stone-carved, tree-like branches at its apex. Organic visions abound in the sanctuary, too, above all sculpted branch and leaflike images. For me, that magnificent church structure told an arboreal story architecturally, which I had mainly grasped only subliminally before. Is it not indeed the case that the great church structures of historic Western Christianity and the great forests of historic Europe were created by the inspiration of the same Spirit?

But much as I have self-consciously and enthusiastically lived with, thought about, and contemplated trees my whole life, and, in particular, often walked the forest path I described in the previous chapter, I have never written at any length about that experience itself. Call this the encounter with treehood (Paul Tillich). That's the story I propose to tell here, joining countless others, of every age, who have also been fascinated with treehood. Along the way, too, I will invite you to recall and to ponder your own soaring and deeply rooted arboreal experiences.

I.

Trees, as you will probably already know, have in recent years become a subject of intense public interest to scholars, nature lovers, novelists, and ecoactivists. The general cultural literature on trees—living with them, celebrating them, understanding them, planting, cultivating, and protecting them—is enormous and shows signs of continuing to grow exponentially.

Perhaps the best-known and most accessible book in this vast recent literature is Peter Wohlleben's 2016 bestseller, *The Hidden Life of Trees.* Also an important part of this global conversation is the widely hailed 2018 novel by Richard Powers, *Overstory* (which I will engage in Chapter 8, below). Interestingly enough, as far as I know, prominent Christian theological and spiritual writers have not been among the leaders in these global discussions.

I want to make my own theological start at reflecting publicly about treehood here, with the hope that these idiosyncratic explorations might prompt others, particularly Christian ecoactivists like yourself, to go and do likewise, in fresh ways. Lord knows, in this era, when forests are being clear-cut or parched out or burned up in many regions of the world, a renewed love for treehood in the US, if we all can work to foster such a passion, could be a blessing for virtually every terrestrial creature, surely for trees themselves, but also for us humans, particularly for the poor who are so vulnerable to the vicissitudes of climate change and other destructive environmental trends.

I want to underline this social justice theme at the outset. Treehood rightly construed has a justice dimension. Sadly, in many poorer city neighborhoods in the US, the tree canopy is thin or virtually nonexistent. This results in higher summer temperatures in those neighborhoods—called urban heat islands—and robs residents of the air filtration and cooling ministries that trees typically provide, not to speak of the trees' more subtle blessings, such as offering opportunities for city dwellers to subliminally engage the wider world of nature in the midst of urban life.

Of course, many cities do have parks, which can make a difference, especially for the poor. While the historical development of green spaces like Central Park in New York City or Boston Commons has been full of socioeconomic ambiguities, the existence of such great parks today—many of them full of grand and gracious trees—in scores of American cities has been a boon for many low-income city dwellers. But that only illustrates, by contrast, why the absence of trees, or the minimizing of their presence, in many

American cities today, has become such a liability. Trees are, indeed, profoundly a justice issue.

Think, too, of the remarkable work of Nobel Laureate Wangari Maathai (1940–2011), who started the Green Belt Movement in Kenya, which has planted more than thirty million trees in order to fight erosion, create firewood, give work to poor women, and generally to work to reestablish the health of the whole biotic community of our planet. Wangari's work presupposed that trees have their own standing: that trees, essentially, are not first and foremost objects for exploitation (whether directly, through commercial exploitation; or indirectly, through the destruction wrought by peoples impoverished in the wake of other kinds of capitalist development). Nor, in Wangari's perspective, are trees essentially a means for the wealthy temporarily to escape from the contradictions and the anomie of modern industrial society under the rubric of ecotourism.

But trees are not only the friends of the poor, as Wangari's example so vividly shows, they are also the lungs of the whole planet, as we often have been told, without which all of us would not for long tangibly live on God's good earth. Each year, trees breathe in almost a quarter of the planet's carbon emissions. They're essential for life on this earth as we know it. (Pray for the Amazon and for the Tsongas in Alaska!)

Beyond all this, trees also are our bonded companions along the way to eternal salvation, theologically speaking. We wouldn't be us without them, now or in the age to come. The eschatological new earth, for which I'm waiting in hope, along with the eschatological new heavens, will surely feature a rich abundance of trees. But I'm getting way ahead of myself. Let me begin at the beginning.

II.

The first tree I ever fell in love with was a Lombard poplar. I grew up in an exurban setting, next to Buffalo, New York. One side of the family land was lined with these tall, cylinder-shaped trees, which had already grown to full height, perhaps sixty feet tall, when I was a child. Typically without my parents knowing, I would on occasion climb up one of those poplars as high as I dared. The branches were fragile, but, for a slim eleven-year-old, that climb was safe; or so I thought back then. On those ascents, I often imagined myself to be a kind of heroic adventurer. I would station myself maybe forty feet above the ground for a spell, as I surveyed our house below and the fields beyond, and feel the wind bending the tree and brushing my face. It was a boy's dream. For those moments, I lived ecstatically in another world, thanks to that poplar tree.

In retrospect, I can imagine that those tree-climbing adventures must have had an important psychological function for me, in addition to everything else. I was an unhappy child at times, a condition that I only began to understand much later when I was in therapy during my college years. High up in one of those trees, I suppose that I was able to leave those psychic tensions behind, if only for a short time.

In therapy, I came to understand that, among other family dynamics, I had had a conflicted relationship with my own father. He was a kind and caring man, but I began to realize that he was also distant at some deeper levels. Enter the world of trees. Perhaps thanks to his German heritage—traditionally, Germans cherished their parks, perhaps more than many ethnic groups—my father loved trees. One of his uncles, who was also of German descent, had had a top position in the Buffalo parks department in the late nineteenth century. That uncle oversaw the implementation of a plan to plant what turned out to be many thousands of sweepingly gracious elm trees, along both sides of many of the city's parkways.

Buffalo in those days came to be a city of green archways. In 1905, it was estimated that Buffalo's street and park trees numbered more than three-hundred thousand, more than one hundred and eighty thousand of them elms. Buffalo was Elm City without the name. Sadly, just about all the elm trees in Buffalo have now died, because of Dutch elm disease. But back then, such trees were a gracious and beautiful promise of the vital life that many of the city's inhabitants wanted to enjoy with each other and with the world around them.

That history behind him, my father often found times to distance himself from his intense professional life—he was a dentist who served an ethnic German neighborhood in the city—by planting trees all around our sizeable exurban land. And he regularly enlisted me to work with him in the planting and the caring processes, which was always a delight for me. Those were some of the times when I truly felt close to him. We planted many fruit trees together and a number of specimen trees, whose names, except for the pin oaks, I cannot now remember. And we cared for those trees together, over the years, watering, manuring, digging around, and pruning them.

III.

Adventurous joy with those poplar climbings by myself and warm personal bonding with those tree plantings and that tree care with my father—those were some of the deeper experiences of my younger years, which I came to cherish as I grew into adulthood. Also, during my high school years, my family had the means to travel to many of the nation's great national parks during extended summer vacations. At that time, just after World War II, those parks typically were not overcrowded as they often are today.

Under my father's tutelage on those trips, I came to affectionately and wondrously encounter many splendid trees that were new to me: the majestic redwoods of California, for sure; also the effervescent quaking aspens of Utah, with their marvelously interconnected roots; and vast stands of towering western hemlocks and red cedars in Glacier National Park.

All this played out for me with an intense love, for the trees and for my father, even as I was, in those my conflicted teenage years, painfully trying to separate myself from him and from the rest of my family. Years later, as I read the works of John Muir, I wondered whether his solitary thousand-mile walk across the South as a young man—and his celebration of many dozens of magnificent trees along the way—was not driven by his intense (perhaps too intense) relationship with his own father, who, with

Bible in hand, had introduced his brilliant son to the glories of God's natural creation. Did son John *have* to make that journey because he *had* to get away from his intensely present father? Or did the father's love for the earth and for its creatures inspire the son to embark on that adventure? Perhaps it was both.

Remarkably for a slow reader like myself, after I had passed my doctoral qualifying exams in theology, I found a way to read every volume of the collected works of John Muir, even though those works were obviously not immediately germane for my chosen field of academic research (twentieth-century German theology). In those days, I had this wonderfully naïve idea that aspiring theologians would as a matter of course read books however the Spirit might move them. The Spirit, I thought back then, had led me to John Muir. In due course, I discovered that the Spirit had also been prompting me to explore the works of Henry David Thoreau.

Usually, I know, students read in the other direction, the more famous Concord sage first, then the lesser known father of US national parks. I think, in retrospect, that I read Muir first, and thoroughly, because he was so deeply imbued with Calvin's theology, whether Muir himself fully understood that or not, and since by that time, I had immersed myself in Calvin's thought, along with Luther's—both of whom, I came to believe and then subsequently to argue in *Brother Earth*, were dedicated champions of the goodness of creation and the glories and the mysteries of the natural world in particular.

I read Muir and Thoreau, ironically perhaps, at the same time when I was working on my doctoral dissertation on the great Karl Barth's—highly problematical—theology of nature. Although Barth offered a stellar reconfiguration of the theologies of Luther and Calvin, his theology as a whole, seminal indeed as it was, never helped me to understand, much less to affirm, my long-standing love for trees. Muir's and then Thoreau's encounters with trees did. The result was a theological proposal, on my part, for a new way to understand my love—or anyone's love—for trees.

IV.

Barth had adopted what was at the time a more or less conventional theological way to understand human relationships with other creatures, a theme developed by many thinkers in his era, but which was most often associated with the name of the Jewish philosopher Martin Buber and his book, *I and Thou*. Buber contrasted an I-Thou relation, which he thought of in intimate, personalistic terms, with an I-It relation, which he defined as an objectifying relationship between a person and a thing.

So, when a woman says to her partner, authentically, "I love you," that's an I-Thou relationship. When she picks up a hammer and hits a nail, that's an I-It relationship. Buber and others (among them Barth) who gave this way of thinking currency in the early twentieth century, were eager to protect and then to celebrate the authenticity of genuine human relationships and to reject any kind of objectifying relationships between humans and other humans. All humans should always be regarded as ends-in-themselves, according to this way of thinking, and should never be treated as objects to be manipulated.

For sure. But what about my relationship with trees? The I-Thou, I-It way of thinking didn't account for my love of trees. Trees are not persons. You cannot communicate with a tree the way you can communicate with your spouse, as a Thou. Are all trees, therefore, in truth mere objects? Was that Lombard poplar which I adored when I was eleven years old merely an object that I used, like a ladder, to climb up into the sky? Or was it, in truth, a creature in its own right, worthy of my respect, even adulation? Wasn't it the case that as a boy I not only clung to that tree, forty feet above ground, for safety's sake, but also to embrace it? To *hug* it?! That tree, for me, back then was no mere object. It was something else. But what? Buber recognized this problem in an appendix to the second edition of *I and Thou*. He even imagined a relationship to a tree that is somehow akin to an I-Thou relationship, but he self-consciously chose not to try to think that through. I decided that I myself would give it a try.

V.

In my first scholarly article in 1968, I argued that a revision of Buber's thought was required. Hence my title: "I-Thou, I-It, and I-Ens." I-Ens? I know that this kind of language might sound esoteric. But not necessarily so. It's as close to you as the glorious sunset refracted over the lake before you or the hummingbird hovering miraculously near to one of the cardinal flowers blossoming in your neighborhood park.

I wrote that article highlighting the idea of an I-Ens relationship, because I wanted to be able to talk about the trees that I loved as ends-in-themselves, no longer as mere objects. In that article, to illustrate I-Ens relationships, I drew attention not only to thinkers such as Thoreau and Muir and their relationships with nature, but also to Luther's and Calvin's visions of earthly creatures. Both Reformers, like Thoreau and Muir, portrayed those creatures in non-objectifying terms and indeed celebrated those creatures as ends in themselves, as, in some sense, charged with the mystery of God. Luther saw miracles in the creatures of nature everywhere and stood in awe of them. Calvin considered the whole of nature to be a theater of Divine glory and celebrated that glory enthusiastically.

In ensuing publications, above all in my study of historic Christian attitudes toward nature, *The Travail of Nature*, I employed the constructs of I-Thou, I-It, *and* I-Ens as a kind of silent interpretive key to open up the whole sweep of classical Christian theology in a new way. I argued there that—notwithstanding Lynn White Jr.'s then widely hailed critique of the Christian tradition as ecologically bankrupt, alleging that Christians have almost always treated nature as a mere object, something to be manipulated—we can trace a major Christian tradition that richly affirms the natural world in its own right.

That way of thinking I could have called the Ens-tradition. Representatives of this ecological tradition, my preferred terminology when I wrote *The Travail of Nature*, were many, I argued. I focused my theological attention particularly on Irenaeus in the second century, the mature Augustine in the fifth century, Saint

Francis in the thirteenth century, and Luther and Calvin in the sixteenth century.

In retrospect, I believe that my reflections about Buber's way of thinking and my historical investigations in *The Travail of Nature* were dependent on my early encounters with treehood. Likewise for my conversion to environmental activism, along the way—ecoactivism, as I later came to think of it. That happened, emphatically, after I first began to work my way through books in the early 1960s that reported the emergence of trends that I and many others had never heard of before—books such as Rachel Carson's *Silent Spring* and Stewart Udall's *The Quiet Crisis*. It was natural, as it were, for me in those days, and subsequently, not only to love trees in their own right, but also to do all that I could do to protect them.

VI.

But my life with trees by no means came to expression just in youthful encounters or in midlife scholarly writings or even in longstanding commitments to ecoactivism. I also have been blessed throughout my life by existential encounters with trees of many kinds. This story, which began in my youth with my father, has more recently unfolded mainly in two places—one in Watertown, Massachusetts, where Laurel and I have lived for more than two decades; the other at Hunts Corner, in rural southwestern Maine, in the foothills of the White Mountains, where we have owned an old farmhouse for more than forty years—behind which I once worked to uncover that forest path I discussed in Chapter 4, above.

Our Watertown apartment building happens to be stationed right next to the justly famous Mount Auburn Cemetery, the country's first and still most beautiful, I believe, of its many striking cemetery-arboretums. Laurel and I often walk around that magnificent place. We celebrate signs of the seasons together, like the first showing of the witch-hazel blossoms in late winter or the delicate, weeping cherry blossoms in the early spring or the images of the gorgeously light-green towering willow trees refracted on the almost still surface of one of the ponds in the summer months.

I once thought that I would try to identify every species of the more than five thousand trees in Mount Auburn, but then I learned that there are more than six hundred different kinds of trees in that cemetery, among them numerous cultivars, so I resolved to focus first on the trees that have been marked by arboretum caretakers with bronze nameplates. But keeping my mind sharp enough to remember the names even of those trees has proved to be a challenge.

One group of trees in Mount Auburn, some of them perhaps a 150 years old or more, has taken on a kind of mythic meaning for Laurel and for me: the gigantic but gracefully arching purple beeches. I have come to recognize them as, for me, the best available natural symbols of Eternal Life on this planet. I can easily see myself sitting on a bench at the edge of a pond in the arboretum for some time (as I have often done), ecstatically contemplating one of those fulsome, towering, dark-leaved creatures on the other side of the pond and its mysterious reflections on the water before me, just as I can easily see myself sitting on a bench for some time in the nave of Chartres Cathedral (as I once did), ecstatically contemplating the glorious stained glass windows high above and the soaring haloed spaces everywhere else.

VII.

Then there's that old farmhouse and its land at Hunts Corner in southwestern Maine. Two hundred years ago, much of New England, including sizeable areas of Maine in particular, had been cleared of forests for the sake of agriculture. Things have changed radically since then. If the truth be known, the trees now own that part of the world. Our fifteen-acre plot is mostly covered by trees—a small part of which is precariously open to us, thanks to the path I described in the previous chapter—and is surrounded by a forest that extends for many miles in every direction. Visible signs of human incursion into that world are few, with the exception of the roads, of course, which is where the houses huddle, and the land that is pierced by the gigantic, underground Portland-to-Montreal oil pipeline, which happens to cut right across our property.

I know little about the history of our land at Hunts Corner. I do know that our area of Maine, before the arrival of European settlers, was the home of the Abenaki people. But as far as I can tell, records of historic Indigenous communities, if there are any, have mostly been suppressed. Hunts Corner apparently has its name from a tavern that used to be located there in colonial times, owned by a family with that name—a waystation for horse-drawn coaches on the road between Portland to the south and Bethel to the north.

Our house, which dates from the mid- to late nineteenth century (according to some maps we've seen), appears to originally have been a large single-room dwelling with a central chimney (the huge foundations of which are still visible in the basement), perhaps with outbuildings. We can tell that there was a sizeable barn constructed next to the house at some early date; remnants of its foundations, huge boulders, still remain.

An ominous cultural memory hovers over all this. Longtime residents in the Hunts Corner area still talk about 1815, the "year without a summer." That was the time when Indonesia's volcano, Mount Tambora, exploded—and drastically changed Maine's weather. Volcanic dust dimmed the rays of the sun. It was a winter during the summer. Crops failed. Livestock died. Famine was always near at hand. Scores of families left the region that year for what they thought would be a much saner and safer life further west. Those who remained must have had good reason to support each other in every way possible.

A sign of this is the Grange building that still exists down the street from us, right at Hunts Corner, just a bit up the road from where the colonial tavern might well have been located. The Grange's roots go back into the nineteenth century. Cooperatives like these must have been necessities, not superfluous cultural artifacts—as this Grange had become by the time Laurel and I first began to put down roots in the area (early on, we were invited by a neighbor to some kind of a Grange ritual involving costumes and some dancing, which we never understood). The Grange now stands empty, a monument to struggles for life itself in years gone by.

Notwithstanding such powerful historical memories, these days, at and around Hunts Corner, the forest still defines everything else, as I have already observed. Yes, you see signs of human habitation along the country road that runs by our house and mud roads running off into the woods here and there. Then there's the ominous pipeline. But this area mainly belongs to the forest I've been talking about. And the forest has surely become, for me, the world I inhabit at Hunts Corner.

Like much of exurban New England, our fifteen acre plot was in all likelihood farmland a hundred fifty years ago. The west side of our land is marked by one of those famous stone walls to which I alluded in the previous chapter. But I have the feeling that our small plot of cleared land only exists today by permission of the forest. I scythe a large swath of our land once a year in the fall. By that time, that area is already crowded with fresh growth, three and four foot tall saplings, which would, if left undisturbed, turn into a rejuvenated extension of the forest in a couple of years. In that part of Maine, we do belong to the trees.

Closer to our house, many different kinds of trees still claim their own places. I have developed friendly relationships over the years with some of them, I-Ens relationships, as I now think about these things. I have learned to call many of those trees by name. When no other humans are around, indeed, I sometimes speak to the trees I know best—"Glad to see you again. How're you doing? That last storm did a number on you, didn't it?"

The oldest trees on our land tend to be near the stone wall I've mentioned or to be growing from an adjacent, steep stony incline, which never could have been farmed. One mother oak in particular has fascinated me ever since I first noticed it. It's enormous. I can't put my arms even halfway around its mammoth base. That poor tree has been hammered and seared over its long lifetime by the elements. The top of its central trunk was apparently sheared off by lightning, perhaps decades ago. But the tree has lived on. Near that mother oak grow a number of smaller, but nevertheless sizeable descendants. I once walked through that area with a neighbor, and he eagerly explained to me that I could make a lot of money if I were to have those oaks cut down for commercial sale.

Grand old towering mother white pines also grow in that area and elsewhere on our land. My brother, Gary, and I once cut down one of those giants after it had died—this for safety reasons. I didn't want it to fall on anyone, particularly on my grandchildren, who sometimes had ventured out near that tree, at the edge of the forest.

Treehood should not be romanticized. A tearful grandfather once told me, in a long, quiet conversation, how he had lost his own daughter to a tree, in the prime of her life. This was the story that onlookers reported. His daughter and her two toddlers had been picnicking in a park, on a very windy day. On their way home, she was watching them run on playfully ahead of her. At one point, she saw a large tree falling down on to the children. She ran desperately to push them out of the way, which she did. But she herself was killed. That story was in my mind, as were my own grandchildren, all the time my brother and I were working to take down that immense but dead pine tree at the edge of our forest. Huge it was. Gary and I barely had the strength together to roll four-foot segments from that tree's trunk into the woods to their final resting places.

Laurel and I are concerned about the future of the pines in our forest. In the forty-odd years that we have owned the land, those great pines seem to have held their own, but they don't seem to be reproducing very well. Likewise for the oaks, notwithstanding their occasional fat years, as they're sometimes called, when all the mature oaks produce acorns in incredible abundance, this, to outsmart the squirrels. For reasons we don't fully understand, we're worried about the oaks, too.

In the meantime, American beeches have moved in everywhere. I once read that these trees can take over a forest, because they don't have to grow underneath openings in the canopy above in order to claim the sunlight that they need to survive. They can send out long branches horizontally to find sunshine filtering through the leaves of other trees and then eventually send their own trunks upward to claim their own space in the canopy. American beeches have even moved into the small woodlot we own across the street from our house, which for the past four decades was populated mainly by ash trees, which somehow managed, over the years, to keep other species out. Not anymore.

VIII.

Early on in our tenure at Hunts Corner, I began to carve out the long winding path in the back forest that I described in the preceding chapter. That's where that mother oak and a number of the great white pines live. That path winds up the slope of those woods, but then winds around back home, not only because it has reached our property line, but also because the ascent thereabouts becomes arduous, in places even treacherous, as nearby Round Mountain (only a hill compared to the White Mountains to the west) makes its rising presence felt. I do everything I can to keep our path in those woods cleared, as I have already noted, in order to keep it safely accessible to us humans.

Closer to our house, I have planted a variety of specimen trees over the years and occasionally cut away competitors, in order to allow some extant trees to flourish. In my mind's eye, I can see the several saplings I once planted near our house years ago, all of them now sizeable trees: the larch, the cedar, the grey birch, the paper birch, the catalpa, and the cherry tree—the last well over forty-five years old now, but still blossoming gorgeously in the spring, notwithstanding its mostly rotted shell of a trunk.

Lately, I have added a large elm sapling to the eastern side of our land, the kind that's supposed to be resistant to Dutch elm disease. As this young tree grows, it will hopefully allow me to hearken back to some of my earliest experiences as a boy. It's planted next to the small stream that runs across our land, near the sole surviving traditional elm tree thereabouts, which towers majestically far above all the other surrounding trees. Gorgeous elm trees, now gone of course, once lined the street in exurbia where I grew up, just as they also once lined the parkways of nearby Buffalo, as I have already observed. As a teenager, I once built a makeshift tree-house in one of those majestic elms.

Perhaps the most striking of all the transplanting that Laurel and I have done over the years was the operation that she and I once performed on what was, for us at the time, a nameless sapling. It was March, early on in our experience with the world of rural Maine. What we did was sheer youthful folly. Laurel had decided at that time, that come the next spring, we would turn over a plot just back of our house, where she would begin to create a perennial garden. But there stood that large sapling right in the middle of that space! Without much thought, we decided that we would try to move that tree—right then.

The ground was frozen at that time of year, of course. I had to use an ax to cut out the ball of the roots. Once it was cut free, we could barely lift that ball out of its earthen socket. Now what? We decided to roll it maybe forty yards to the western side of our land. There, using the ax again, and a pickax, I hollowed out a cavity for that big, frozen root ball. Finally, we were able to slide that sapling and the mass of its frozen roots into that hole and to pry some soil free enough to cover those roots.

It was only then that we realized that we had planted that little tree close to the church next door, a pristine white wooden building just up from the Grange. That church easily could have appeared on some New England calendar cover. But that was that. Never mind that sapling. The church building appeared to be as picturesque as ever. We hurried on into the house to warm ourselves by the Franklin Stove.

Little did we know back then that that nameless sapling, more than forty years later, would magically turn into a graceful and flowingly expansive red maple whose sumptuous branches would then completely cover our vista of the whole church building! That iconic structure is gone from our angle of vision for the better part of the year. There may be a parable hidden in this ironic tale, but, if so, I have yet to discover what it is.

IX.

Sadly, the sugar maple I planted at the front of our property many years ago recently died. Sugar maples grow all over our area, so why not there? I hypothesize that that tree, which reached maybe fifty feet in height, gradually succumbed to the salt or salt-like chemicals poured by county trucks on to the road during the winter. The snowplows then throw the snow on to the side of the road and those snowbanks eventually melt and leave the salty stuff to poison the soil. It was painful for me to observe that large and lovely tree die over the course of several seasons and then to witness it standing there, barren, a skeleton.

True, stories like these sometimes have a blessed ending, according to one of the central themes of the Christian faith: from death comes life. We would of course cut down that dead sugar maple and then saw it and split it and stack it for firewood. Over the many years that we have lived at Hunts Corner, we have used our old iron stove in the kitchen steadily, sometimes even on cool summer nights. And we obtain fuel for those fires almost always from standing deadwood, as we say, which we cut down at various places on our land and then drag in, cut up, split, and stack. That was to be the story of that dead sugar maple. We would give thanks for it one more time, so I thought, as it would later warm both our kitchen and our hearts.

But that dead sugar maple's transition to firewood was not as smooth as I had anticipated. That project turned out to be an adventure.

For decades, my brother and I have helped each other with forest and other chores at our respective rural homes; his is in western Connecticut. He learned to love trees the same way I did, working with our father on the grounds of our exurban Buffalo home. After various childhood and adolescent skirmishes, some of them harsh, Gary and I have remained close over the years and have grown even closer in these our golden years, especially by assisting each other in Connecticut or in Maine, for days at a time. I think that I need him more than he needs me in this respect, however, because his forestry experience has been much more extensive than mine. This was one of those cases.

That towering dead sugar maple had to be cut so that it would fall *away* from the street, not *onto* the street, where it might block or even hit some speeding car passing by. With some anxiety, I admit, I nevertheless trusted Gary to cut that tree just so that it would fall precisely where it was supposed to. I had witnessed Gary "place" (his term) falling trees in just the right locations many times.

When this tree began to undulate, however, it did not immediately fall away from the street as Gary had cut it to fall. The tree just stood there trembling, not falling in any direction! What was going to happen? With some sense of urgency (!), and with a long rope tying my brother to that oh-so-perilously undulating tree as it was readying itself to fall in one direction or another, Gary dashed to a spot far away from the street and then pulled on the rope, again and again and again, until the tree finally began to fall toward him (it crashed down a few feet from where he had been standing!) and not onto some unsuspecting car that might have been speeding up or down our road. Quite a feat for one who was at that time about to turn eighty! As I am constantly aware, trees are not always our friends. But thankfully, in this case, Gary was able to coax that tree in a friendly direction, narrowly escaping injuring himself or anyone else.

X.

I have saved for last what is for me the best news about treehood. Not too far from the field by the street where that dead sugar maple finally fell, lies what Laurel and I have called our Hidden Garden. It's a place of repose for us in the green seasons, with a wood swing crafted by Shakers, some rugged rosebushes, and native plantings here and there, backing up against several towering ash trees. Behind the swing, is a row of highbush cranberries, which many years ago I planted with shoots I hacked from a mother bush not too far away. (Laurel has made luscious jelly from their tart red berries, now and again.)

For most of the year, if you were to stand by the stump of the maple tree that my brother and I cut down so adventurously, you wouldn't be able to catch sight of our Hidden Garden, only a stone's throw away. Because—it's hidden! Your view would be blocked by well-grown lilac bushes, a large mock-orange bush, and a huge wild rosebush whose name neither Laurel nor I can ever remember. But come with me now, circuitously, as I take you the long way around to see what for me is the Tree of Life, in the midst of that garden.

Many years ago, Laurel and I purchased a then eight-foot-tall purple beech sapling, and planted it in our Hidden Garden. Long before that, as I've already observed, we had come to adore the gigantic hundred-year-old purple beeches we had encountered in Mount Auburn Cemetery. In this finite world, as I've likewise already commented, those great trees are, for me, the best natural symbols of Eternal Life that I can imagine. Laurel and I have decided to have our ashes interred at the base of our own purple beech, which now towers high above us in the Hidden Garden.

I've affixed a foot-high Celtic cross—made of concrete—at the base of our purple beech, which one day will not only mark the place of our buried ashes but will also announce the Truth, for those who have ears to hear, that has claimed my own soul self-consciously since the first days of my theological study to these my octogenarian years, predicated on a reading of Colossians 1:15 and following—the crucified and risen Lord is *the Cosmic Christ,* both now and forever: "All things have been created through him and for him. He himself is before all things, and in him all things hold together" (Colossians 1:16–17).

I read that cosmic witness to Jesus Christ in the figures and designs on the historic Celtic crosses that I encountered during a trip to Ireland with Laurel in 1996, along with throngs of other spiritual seekers. I concluded then that the classical Celtic saints were by no means just nature mystics, as many who have been fascinated with them in our time have believed. No, their spirituality of nature was consistently a celebration of the cross and resurrection, understood as a revelation of the world to come. For the great Celtic saints, the love of the seas and the earth and its creatures, and the love of Jesus Christ crucified and risen from the dead is the same love.

Hence I was overjoyed when I found and then was able to buy that concrete Celtic cross at Home Depot for $14.98. I eagerly carried it off to implant it in the earth next to the purple beech in our Hidden Garden. I wanted to announce that someone believes—or that someone, whose ashes are interred there, once did believe—that that tree, marked by that Cross, is—or was—for that believer the Tree of Life.

Informed by that experience, I invite you to take the time to bond ever more intensely with the trees in your own world. Perhaps you will even join me (if you have not already done so) in talking to them now and again, when no one else is around. Perhaps you might even venture to find your own Tree of Life and then to dream dreams and see visions of the new heavens and the new earth promised in the words of our biblical forebears.

6

Hearing Nature's Voices
The Mysteries of a Cattail Pond and a Snowshoe Hare

Not far from our old farmhouse in southwestern Maine, where that purple beech I just talked about is growing, and where I sculpted that winding forest path I also have described along the way, there's a little pond full of cattails right at the edge of the road. Most of the year passersby hardly notice it. But on some spring evenings just about no one can miss it. At that time of the year, it's full of tiny frogs; spring peepers they're called. If you were to hold one of those animals in your hand, you'd be astonished. It measures under an inch and a half. It has smooth brownish gray skin, with a dark cross on its back. Which makes these little creatures, when they're in that cattail pond, mostly invisible to human eyes.

In the spring, however, those peepers are, as I've said, unavoidable. Sometimes when I drive by that little pond on an early spring evening, I'll stop the car, roll down all the windows, and just listen. It's symphonic! Dare I say, bombastic? All the males are singing a shrill cacophony. You can hear a full chorus of these tiny frogs maybe a half mile away.

What's going on? Mating, of course. And who's listening? The female spring peepers, I would imagine, unless that's a masculine conceit on my part. *I'm* certainly listening, with amazement! Is *God* listening, too? Even more, could it be that in addition to everything else, those many hundreds of peepers in that little pond are *praising God*? Anyone familiar with the Psalms is likely to be aware that ancient Israel's hymnody is full of references to nature praising God.

Is this just some kind of poetic license? Nature praising God and God hearing nature singing? I want to try to convince you now, if you need convincing, that there's more than meets the ear here, that there's a valuable gift of the biblical imagination right before your very ears—and that it's yours for the hearing. If you don't need convincing, come with me anyway, to hear what you can hear, hopefully to deepen your understanding of this biblically attested experience.

I want to alert you at the outset, too, that in order to do justice to the richness of the witness of the Bible in this respect I will also explore some of the meanings of what I take to be—brace yourself—the *two* voices of nature: not just *the praising* but also *the groaning*. In biblical perspective, the two go together. Yes, this is a challenging thought. But our experience of nature itself is complicated. The faith witness of the Bible is no less complex.

This is where I want to take you. We humans experience nature most fundamentally, I will suggest, in two ways: in terms of its *creativity* and its *destructivity*. I will also suggest that *God* hears that creativity and that destructivity as nature praising God and as nature groaning to God; and therefore so can people of faith, in fragmentary ways.

I.

To describe these experiential and biblical complexities as clearly as I can, I want to say something first about a theme that has already preoccupied us: anthropocentrism. Understandably, theologians, ethicists, spiritual writers, philosophers, professional ecologists, and many other authors and activists have in recent decades taken to railing against human-centered readings of nature. Frequently, this denunciation has taken the form of a passionate rejection of a spectrum of inherited approaches to biblical interpretation, especially the idea of human dominion over nature.

Call this the critical ecological wisdom of our era. And claim this wisdom we must, on theological, ethical, spiritual, and biblical grounds. Thankfully, Pope Francis has told us precisely that in his encyclical, *Laudato Si'*: "We [humans] have come to see ourselves as [mother earth's] lords and masters, entitled to plunder her at will." But: "Clearly, the Bible has no place for a tyrannical anthropocentrism unconcerned for other creatures" (*Laudato Si'*, paragraphs 2 and 68).

Yet, as prophetic denunciations sometimes tend to be, this kind of critique has often been clearer about what is to be rejected than about what is to be affirmed. Anthropocentrism is bad. But what is good? At this point, a number of prophetic voices sometimes seem to have faltered. What is needed, I believe, is some solid teaching across the ecumenical spectrum about what I have called over the years, beginning with *Brother Earth* in 1970, "the integrity of nature."

Which is to say, in the greater scheme of things, nature has its own value and its own status before God. On the one hand, nature is not another name for God, nor, more particularly, as some theologians have argued in recent decades, is nature another name for God's body. Nature is nature. It's a creature in its own right. It has its own standing. Nature doesn't have to be Divine or God's body in order to have its own importance. On the other hand, neither are the creatures of nature merely means to human ends. Nature doesn't have to be subordinated to human life to have meaning. Nature isn't merely the stage for human history (Emil Brunner). Nor is it merely "the means of production" (Karl Marx). Nature is good in itself, and so established and blessed by God.

This is no less true when nature is claimed for human purposes. Imagine that some entrepreneur discovered that spring peepers could become, as it were, a cash crop. Imagine that those tiny frogs could be farmed, as catfish sometimes are. Imagine, further, that they could be harvested and ground up into a kind of nutritious flour to be fed, say, to farm animals. If you drove by such a peepers farm some spring evening, which had large ponds to grow those tiny creatures, and you heard all those millions and millions singing their hearts out, as it were, would that immense song coming from the farmed peepers be of less importance than the song of the wild peepers in the small rural cattail pond, whose serenade I hear from time to time?

I think not. The song of the spring peepers is the song of the spring peepers, heard by God wherever that song comes from, however many frogs there are, and whatever the fate of any of those creatures eventually might be. Those spring peepers have standing in themselves, a divinely bestowed integrity, biblically speaking, even if in addition, somehow, they might also have some human use.

Now I return to my overall theological point: How are we to celebrate the integrity of those spring peepers and avoid devaluing their integrity? It appears to me that we could avoid devaluing the peepers if we understood them to somehow be divine or part of God's body. But do they really have to be divine in order to have their own standing? Likewise, if someone were to view those creatures' standing solely in terms of their production value, if any, in that case, the spring peepers would be robbed of their intrinsic value also. Is there a way to identify the integrity of those spring peepers theologically, beyond simply stating that that's the case?

Turns out that the Scriptures provide an answer for this kind of question. The Scriptures take it for granted that *nature has a voice of its own*—or more than one voice—as we now will see. The Scriptures, in effect, invite us to imagine *God listening* to the voices of the spring peepers. The Scriptures thus invite us, in this concrete manner, to celebrate the integrity of all the creatures of nature.

II.

Wait. Is this real? Nature has voices? And God hears them? And we somehow are to hear them, too? Does this make any theological or any other kind of sense? I believe that it does—but that it takes the investment of some imagination to grasp these matters. I invite you now to think about these complexities in historical terms.

In a prescientific world, people apparently could readily imagine nature praising God and God, in some sense, hearing. When Saint Francis preached to the birds, his biographer tells us, it was to encourage them to communicate their praises to God all the more, to the end, presumably, that God might rejoice in those praises even more. But in our scientific world, how are we to imagine that the creatures of nature have their own voices that are heard by God? To begin to respond to this highly complex question, I want to make several observations.

First—and here we return to a familiar theme, but invoked in an unusual way—it is necessary to address the anthropocentrism often given with the question itself. For too long, in my view, Christians have understood the theme of the Divine hearing primarily in terms having to do with humans only.

Here's a question: Does God hear *your* prayers? Many believers have assumed, as a matter of fiducial fact, that *God does hear our—human!—prayers and praises,* as when we say with Jesus, "Our Father in heaven . . ." Or when we sing with the sensibilities of a Saint Francis, "All creatures of our God and King . . ."

Most of the faithful are also well accustomed, in this process, to the sound of their own voices, praying or singing, especially during the great festivals of the faith, such as Christmas and Easter. The faithful generally assume that God hears *their* supplications and *their* exclamations as they speak and sing in worship. Presumably, to continue same line of thought, God is also multilingual: God hears humans' prayers, we believers typically assume, no matter what language is being spoken—even, on occasion, when God hears what is called speaking in tongues. But is that all?

If God heard the groanings of my wife in the hospital, when each of our two children were being born in 1969 and 1971, as I believe God did—in this case, hers were wordless cries to God of prayerful endurance and prayerful hope—who am I to say that God does not also hear the groaning of a female giraffe in the African wilds, when she drops her newborn six feet to the earth? Wouldn't it be obvious anthropocentrism to say that God hears only the groaning of a human mother in travail?

The spiritual premise here, of course, is our faith that God *does hear* our *cries for mercy and* our *sounds of praise when we utter* our *prayers.* If we believe *that*, therefore, why should we restrict God's hearing just to us humans? Is God only a part-time God of hearing, as it were, or doesn't God hear the outcries of all the creatures? In a word, the theme of the Divine hearing, as it is widely understood in our churches, must be thoroughly revised. Otherwise, we are left with an anthropocentric image of a God who hears only the voices of human creatures.

Second, the image of *God* hearing—anyone or anything—is of course *metaphorical.* Yes, we could imagine different kinds of sounds that God could hear and we humans could not hear—in the same way we know that dogs can hear ranges of sounds that we humans cannot. We could entertain the thought, too, that God can hear the songs of the great whales through the waters over many miles, for example, which we modern humans, without special technologies, cannot hear—although some native peoples do hear many more sounds in nature, such as the songs of the whales, than contemporary Westerners can.

But upon closer examination, it is clearly the case that all such thoughts are dependent on the metaphor of the Divine hearing, including the notion of God hearing human prayers. Note well, God doesn't have eardrums! God's hearing is metaphorical. It's not literal. If we are dealing with a metaphor here, as we are, why then restrict it just to humans?

Third, God's hearing—as we think of it now, metaphorically—is not just restricted to sounds that we humans *might* hear if *we* had the right technologies or the right kind of cultural formation.

In the history of evolution on planet Earth, God listened when the morning stars sang together in the days when the planet was just emerging, when, marauding around the new-born Earth, primeval beasts roared for their prey, when the great sea monsters communicated with one another in the depths of the seas, when the birds and the insects of aboriginal jungles sang forth, each in its own way, their cacophony of sounds. And this all happened long before human creatures had arrived on the scene. God heard it all.

Even today, far from unaided human hearing (but brought to our ears through exquisite technology), elephants make what sound like contented murmurs as they gather in communal space, for a time free from predators and from the demands of foraging. But God hears them. On Mount Saint Victoire a nightingale sings in a dark glade where earlier in the day Cezanne had been painting, and God hears her. The gibbons of Indonesia, mates for life, lift up complex sunrise songs, and whether humans are in range or not, God hears them.

In this sense, when a tree falls in the forest, there *is* sound, even though no humans—or human recording devices—are present, because *God hears*. And, of course, God is able to hear much more than that tree in its particular earthly setting. God's hearing is not just terrestrial. God heard when the big bang happened, something very distantly akin, I imagine, to a human hearing of Beethoven's Ninth Symphony. God hears when a planet is sucked into oblivion in its host star, as planet Earth will be in five billion years, something very distantly akin, I imagine, to a human hearing of Mozart's *Dies Irae*. God hears when infinitesimal, subatomic particles collide or pass through each other in every corner of the universe, in all of its billions of galaxies, something very distantly akin, I imagine, to a human hearing of a Bach fugue.

Fourth, as I have suggested, the notion of nature's voices makes theological sense, not in itself, but because that theme presupposes that *God hears* those voices. If God hears those voices, they must be there to be heard! And then there's this: The theme of God hearing makes theological sense all the more so because it presupposes that *God discloses* that Divine hearing to us in the community of faith, where we humans, when we are so inspired, are existentially taken hold of by the biblical witness to that Divine hearing.

The theme of the voices of nature is therefore first and foremost God centered (*theocentric*), not human centered (*anthropocentric*). We humans, when we are so inspired, are graciously and spiritually moved to join in and, in some fragmentary manner, to listen to the primal voices of nature *as heard by God*, apart from anything we can do or say or think on our own.

III.

But a clarification is in order. I've been considering what I have called the voices of nature to this point, alluding on occasion to the biblical theme of nature praising God. Actually, if we attend more closely to the witness of the Scriptures, we will encounter a more particular theme that I mentioned at the outset: nature has *two* voices!

There's the theme of nature *praising* God that we meet in the Psalms, which has drawn most of my attention to this point. Then there's the theme of the *groaning* of the whole creation that we meet most dramatically in the eighth chapter of Paul's Letter to the Romans. I've alluded to this theme when I recalled my wife in childbirth and a female giraffe in the process of giving birth.

The groaning of the whole creation appears to be a self-authenticating theme. Reinhold Niebuhr was wont to observe that original sin is the only empirically demonstrable Christian truth. Perhaps we could broaden Niebuhr's dictum to include the groaning of the whole creation. It appears to be obvious. There's so much suffering in nature, near and far! So much torrential and tormented violence! If we step back and survey not just human history, but the whole history of life on planet Earth, we soon begin to contemplate a vast picture of "nature, red in tooth and claw" (Alfred, Lord Tennyson). Think of this as *the destructivity of nature*.

At the very end, moreover, according to the projections of some cosmological physicists, the whole universe is destined for a vast collapse of some horrendous kind, perhaps some universal slowdown to a dead frigidity. After countless eons during which many billions of galaxies will have come into being and died, together with all their stars and planets and other astral bodies and particles, infinitely large and infinitely small, everything in the universe will have come to an end (*finis*), a kind of universal, grinding cosmic halt. Not "Love Supreme" (John Coltrane), but Death Supreme will reign at the very end of our cosmos as we know it today, scientifically. Destructivity, therefore, is indeed a key construct we can invoke to describe the "Great Story" (Thomas Berry) of our universe, since its first moments to the ending of all things, as we know that narrative from the findings of the natural sciences.

But destructivity, it almost goes without saying, is not the only grand truth about the universe, as we know it, again, with the help of the natural sciences. From what is called the big bang to the formation of galaxies and the emergence of countless planets and then life on at least one of those planets, ours, the Great Story of the universe is also the unfolding of an amazing *creativity*.

The Catholic paleontologist and theologian Pierre Teilhard de Chardin described this process richly in terms of the root meaning of *genesis*. For Teilhard, the whole universe has evolved through a series of creative evolutionary stages of coming-into-being: cosmogenesis, biogenesis, noogenesis (*noo* for "mind" or "consciousness"), and Christogenesis, drawn forth in every instance by the creative and quasi-magnetic force of the Cosmic Christ. Working with much more secular assumptions, the Protestant philosophical theologian Gordon Kaufman identified the immense creativity of the universe *with God*. God, for Kaufman, *is*—creativity. And creativity is God. But however it is construed, creativity is doubtless a key construct, along with destructivity, for helping us to grasp the mysteries and the complexities and the glories and the tragedies of the Great Story of our universe.

IV.

The biblical narratives of the second voice of nature, the groaning, to which I now turn, appear to be closely related to the aforementioned, experienced realities of destructivity. This is not the place to undertake a comprehensive survey of the biblical theme, the groaning of the whole creation. I will consider here, in short compass, the preeminent biblical passage pertaining to that theme, Romans 8:18–23, particularly as it allows us to understand in some measure what for faith is the groaning of the creatures of nature.

This is a highly compact and complicated text, which advocates of ecological theology have sometimes oversimplified or overinterpreted. I will focus on these words: "We know that the whole creation has been groaning in labor pains until now" (Romans 8:22).

I begin with some comments about the historical context of these words. Although Paul is preoccupied in his Letter to the Romans with a number of particular issues in the church of his time, above all with the relationship between Jews and Gentiles, *Paul also presupposes two grand narratives:*

1. The *first grand narrative* is the story of the rise and the power of *Rome* and its claims for ultimacy.
2. The *second grand narrative* is the story of the world's creation, human sin, the redemption of humans, and finally the consummation of the whole cosmos, the narrative of the biblical *God's* ultimacy.

The first story was celebrated by the classical Roman poet Virgil. He announced the dawning of a golden age in the reign of Caesar Augustus. But as the apostle Paul and the Roman Christians to whom he wrote would have known well, the facts on the ground radically belied such imperial propaganda. The Roman Empire was a ruthless, militaristic culture predicated on slave labor and vast exploitations of nature. In particular, both Paul and his audience, as New Testament scholar Robert Jewett has observed, could well have thought about how imperial ambitions, military conflicts, and economic exploitations had led to the erosion of the natural environment throughout the Mediterranean world, leaving ruined cities, depleted fields, deforested mountains, and polluted streams.

Roman culture was also undergirded by the violent cult of animal sacrifice in most major cities of the empire. We know that early Christian writers, surrounded by this pervasive culture of bloody sacrifice, engaged in a vigorous polemic *against* ritual killing and its violence. Still, such animal sacrifice was a routine part of Roman life. Violence in general and violence against animals in particular made the Roman world go 'round. This was no golden age.

Hence the expression "the groaning of the whole creation" (see Romans 8:22) was in all likelihood implicitly linked, for Paul, with the desecration of the earth by the powerful and a culture of violence more generally—violence against animals and slaves and subjugated peoples as well as against forests and fields and rivers.

Ample evidence in biblical traditions would have inclined Paul and other first-century Christians to believe that this situation presupposed what *for us* might be thought of as a divinely mandated feedback loop: God judges human sinfulness in part at least by "cursing the ground" (Genesis 3:14–19) because of the violent deeds of sinful humans like Cain. In response to human sin, in other words, God reshapes the human experience in nature so that that experience is no longer just the blessing that God had intended it to be, but also a curse, especially under the tyranny of Roman power. This is why, at least in part, according to this way of thinking, creation groans.

It appears, furthermore, that the motif of creation groaning brings with it some reference to a kind of suffering that is endemic to nature, apart from the interventions by the powers of Rome that were so disruptive and well-known, and apart from human sin more generally. Consider, in this respect, the end-time expectations of many first-century Christians. Those hopes were shaped, in some measure at least, by the prophecies of Isaiah, which envisioned the messianic age to come as a time of cosmic peace, a time when "the wolf shall live with the lamb, / the leopard shall lie down with the kid, / the calf and the lion and the fatling together, / and a little child shall lead them." (Isaiah 11:6) This is the world, according to the biblical imagination, that is to replace the current earthly cosmos and its violence in every corner.

First-century Christians would also have known about the promise of cosmic peace that was popularly associated with emperors such as Augustus and *their* alleged golden age. This was thought to be a peace that presupposed the ending of violence toward and among animals, not unlike the peace announced by the prophecies of Isaiah.

Read in this context, it appears that "the groaning of the whole creation" also would have been understood by Paul and his readers as in some respects referring to the suffering wrought by nature-on-nature violence, as well as the suffering brought about by human-on-nature and human-on-human violence. With the arrival of the End Times, that kind of violence will be over, too. No longer will the wolf eat the lamb.

It seems clear, too, that the expression "the groaning of the whole creation" presupposes that *God hears* that groaning. Such an observation is strengthened when we examine the word Paul uses for "groaning." It calls to mind traditional mourning practices of Paul's Jewish heritage, which were often replete with loud cries of grieving in the company of others. Paul, as a matter of course, attributes the same kind of intense emotional expressivity in a communal setting to the groaning of *all* the creatures. All the creatures cry aloud because of their misery! Paul seems to have had a real, public expression of universal grief in mind—which humans can and do hear—predicated on the firmly held conviction that God hears all those cries of grief. Such, in broad outline, is Paul's understanding of the groaning of the creation.

V.

Now let's return to the biblical theme that I've alluded to since the outset of this discussion: nature praising God. Most of the biblical calls to nature to praise God are found in the Psalms and are rooted in the practices of worship. Psalm 148 is perhaps the best case in point. This psalm was used daily for centuries in monasteries throughout the West. It undoubtedly helped shape a major—ecological—strain in Western Christian theology and spirituality. Saint Francis, for one, sang this psalm every day at the devotional hour of Lauds; and it was in all likelihood much on his mind and in his heart when he composed his Canticle of the Creatures.

In Psalm 148 the language of worship takes over. Psalm 148 is a ritual itinerary of the whole creation, immersed in the creation traditions of ancient Israel, spoken from the context of the temple liturgy. Heavenly creatures are called upon to praise God, then sun and moon and stars, and "the waters above the heavens" (vv. 1–4). Next the primal realities of the earth are invited to join in: "sea monsters and all deeps, fire and hail, snow and frost, stormy wind fulfilling [God's] command" (vv. 7–8). Every creature of nature is to have its part: "Mountains and all hills, fruit trees and all cedars! / Wild animals and all cattle, creeping things and flying birds" (vv. 9–10)! Humans of every rank and age are also asked to join in the song of the whole creation (vv. 11–12). Finally, the psalm comes to a kind of frenzied rest with the cultic affirmation of "the name of [Yahweh]" in the midst of the people called to praise that name. As they lift up their voices with the whole creation, they stand in awe before God, who is "the horn" of their salvation (vv. 13–14), "horn" here being a figure for immense and transcendental power.

VI.

How, then, do we bring these biblical themes about *nature groaning* and *nature praising* into the conversation we moderns sometimes entertain about *the destructivity* and *the creativity* of nature? From a theological perspective I want to propose a relatively simple answer to that question, an answer that I signaled at the outset. As people of faith, we—our minds and hearts—are shaped by the witness of the Scriptures and by our worship practices during which we hear that witness and then respond, especially with hymnic affirmations like Saint Francis's Canticle of the Creatures.

I believe, then, that inspired by the Spirit, we can entertain this judgment: *God hears what we in our era consider to be the destructivity and the creativity of nature—as nature groaning before God and as nature offering its praises to God.*

The presupposition here, as I have said, is clearly that *God* hears those voices. What is more, as God hears the destructivity of nature as nature's groaning and the creativity of nature as nature's praising, we who participate by faith in the worship of God's household can join in the hymn of the whole creation—in the sounds of groaning and in the sounds of praising—both with a knowing passion and with a critical awareness of how fragile our understandings of these Divine matters actually are.

VII.

Are, then, the spring peepers in that cattail pond praising God? I believe that insofar as I am immersed in the worship of the household faith, where the Scriptures are faithfully interpreted and where I can sing my heart out in response to that interpretation, I can answer Yes to that question. Singing hymns like Saint Francis's Canticle of the Creatures, and singing them enthusiastically, helps to shape my mind and heart so that I can have flashes of insight about myself praising God at that moment *with* the voices of all God's creatures.

What then about the groaning of all the creatures? The same logic of worship would seem to apply here, to help us answer this question, but even more cautiously. If it is the case, as I believe it is, that God hears what for us is the descriptively discernible creativity of nature as the nature's praise, and if likewise God hears what for us is the descriptively discernible destructivity of nature as nature's groaning, we humans, insofar as we join in worship of this God and hear this God's Word, can also be attuned, in some manner, to hear that groaning, much as we are attuned to hear nature's creatures praising God.

The difference between the two experiences for us (the groaning and the praising) seems to be this. Apart from natural disasters like floods or hurricanes or tsunamis, which, variously, overcome us, much of nature's destructivity occurs either beyond our ken or when we are trying to escape from it. Destructivity typically is not an experience that allows us to rest and to contemplate—apart from the somewhat distanced observations of some natural scientists (the thought, say, of our sun being swallowed by the black hole at the center of our galaxy someday), or the distant encounters of some mountain hikers today, who can on rare occasions hear the thunderous fall of tons of ice resounding from a glacier across a Swiss valley. Typically, it seems, we humans are prone to *withdraw* before the face of natural destructivity, even to flee, if we possibly can. The most recent and perhaps most poignant example of this has been the sequestering at home many of us have experienced during the COVID-19 crisis.

The psalmist attests to this kind of experience in descriptions of wild animals at night, saying of the Creator God,

> You make darkness, and it is night,
>> when all the animals of the forest come creeping out.
> The young lions roar for their prey,
>> seeking their food from God.
> When the sun rises, they withdraw
>> and lie down in their dens.
> People go out to their work
>> and to their labor until the evening. (Psalm 104:20–23)

We humans know the destructivity of nature, which God hears as nature's groaning. But we only rarely encounter that destructivity in its full and awesome power in a way that allows us to hear it as momentously as God does—as groaning.

VIII.

All of this brings me back to that rural road in southwestern Maine, to that cattail pond where I can, in season, hear the charged nightly song of the spring peepers. They may be "raising hell," as I once heard one of my Maine neighbors say. But theologically speaking, they're raising heaven—on earth. Theirs is a beautiful song of praise as God hears it—and as we can hear it imaginatively, too, in some small measure, with the ears of faith.

And the groaning of the creatures? I have referred along the way to a female giraffe dropping her newborn in the wilds, and I also alluded historically to the practices of bloody animal sacrifice in ancient Rome. Those thoughts, especially the latter, cause me to shudder. But here, at the very end of this discussion, I want to share with you a story of what is for me a still more personal and therefore more sobering encounter. To that end, I would like to take you with me to that selfsame road, alongside of which that cattail pond is located.

Walking along that road a short distance from that pond early one morning, I once witnessed what to me was a most painful sight. I began to approach what appeared to be a dead animal lying on the pavement. That it was. Apparently it had been struck by some vehicle during the night, but since that road is not heavily traveled during those hours, the body was firm and intact. It had not been pummeled by other cars or trucks.

The animal lying dead there looked to me to be a large and elegant rabbit, of a size I had never seen before. Only when I later returned home and did some investigating did I learn that it was not a rabbit, strictly speaking. It was a snowshoe hare, almost never seen by us humans, since these animals are mainly nocturnal creatures. As I approached that dead form, not knowing then what kind of an animal it might be, I stopped and contemplated its elegance. It was surely not the kind of rabbit that typically scampered around back home, eating clover, in Mount Auburn Cemetery.

At that moment, knowing only that this, for me, was an extraordinary sight, I slowly put on my work gloves and carefully picked up that still vital form—so it felt to me—and carried it a few yards into the woods. I couldn't bear the thought of more cars or trucks running over that beautiful body, again and again and again, during the day. I covered that dead rabbit-like creature that

I was later to learn was a snowshoe hare with some fallen branches; and then I again stood there silently for some moments.

Had that elegant creature groaned when it was struck on that road in the night? If so, I was sure that God had been there and that God had heard that groaning, just as God was there with Jesus on the cross and had heard Jesus's groaning, when Jesus had cried out with a loud voice, "My God, my God, why have you forsaken me?"

I invite you to give yourself permission to rest, however painfully, in such experiences. With other Christian ecoactivists and coworkers of good will, you are struggling to help save a planet full of an anguish that's been exacerbated excruciatingly by human interventions. It's good for your soul, on occasion, to allow yourself to feel that anguish, in whatever form you might be encountering it—whether on a country road facing a dead snowshoe hare or downtown next to a coal-fired power plant that's been belching hot poisons into the air for many years, which humans (especially the poor) and other creatures breathe over the long term, likely hastening the day of their demise.

The groaning of the whole creation is all around us. But that's by no means all, according to the witness of the Scriptures. Sensing this in faith, if you choose, you yourself—driven by the Spirit in a wrenching act of faith—will be enabled, once your own groaning has for a time run its course, to join enthusiastically with the whole creation praising the biblical God of hope, who has promised to make all the crucified creatures of this world new, one day, eternally.

7

Seeing Nature through a Glass Darkly

Niagara Falls and Our Sublimely Natural God

This should not be a surprise. Christian ecoactivists believe in God. That goes with the territory of being people of faith, of course. But which God? Most Christian ecoactivists, by my observation, take the primary narratives of the Scriptures for granted, above all the vision of God as the Creator and Redeemer of all things, the grand story of the Bible, from the book of Genesis through the Psalms and the story of Jesus to the book of Revelation. Most Christian ecoactivists, more particularly, believe in the God announced by the Gospel of John—the God who loves the cosmos, everykind—not just humankind and surely not just mankind.

But I think that you who are Christian ecoactivists have an advantage in this respect, which you may not always consciously recognize. You are acquainted with nature. You love nature, in your own way. That's why Saint Francis may well be your patron saint, as he is mine. You are therefore regularly ready to encounter God in a way that may seem *natural* to you—in more than one sense of that word—but which others less attuned to the grandeur and the complexities of nature may not be. You are in a position to contemplate God in nature—to invoke the language of the apostle Paul (1 Corinthians 13:12 KJV)—"as through a glass darkly," but you can still *see*, in a deeper spiritual sense. This is another way that you are a gift to the whole church, quite beyond your leadership in ecoactivist struggles.

I want to help you now to discover more self-consciously what probably you already experientially know. To that end, I will once again speak in terms of my own story—yet with the following questions in mind every step of the way. Isn't this the way *you* see God, too? Don't *you* also believe in a sublimely natural God? Along the way, I'll also take you to Niagara Falls.

I.

At the start, we are well-advised to identify or to recall a certain narrowness in some of the church's teachings about God, for much of its history. Traditionally, Christians have often privileged spirit over nature. This has sometimes been called a *spirit-matter dualism.*

According to this way of thinking, things spiritual are good and things material are of lesser value—even, from some perspectives (such as that of historical Gnosticism, a faith tradition rejected by a variety of Christian theologians of various periods), of profoundly negative value. The result has been a tendency at key junctures in the Christian tradition to devalue the world of nature as a whole and the human body in particular, and to understand God as radically separate and thoroughly different from the material world of creation.

More than a few Christians today, along with an array of critics of the Christian tradition, just assume that this is how *all* Christians have thought about the natural world throughout the ages. Nature for Christians, it has regularly been alleged, is something inferior, even dangerous, signified by the expression "the sins of the flesh." This is why my theme may sound strange to some. A sublimely natural God? Isn't such a notion contrary to the Bible itself? Doesn't the Gospel of John announce that "God is spirit"

(John 4:24)? How could any reputable Christian speak of God in terms of nature?

But note first that the Gospel writer himself in all likelihood understood "spirit" here to mean "the Spirit" and, indeed, "the Spirit of the Creator"—as that theme is attested in Genesis 1:2, where we see the Spirit of the Creator hovering over the primeval waters of a creation-coming-into-being, a critically important interpretive insight for us today. But it is also true, historically, that this *text* from John in due course came to serve as a *pretext* for a fundamental shift of meaning in the first Christian centuries and, increasingly, thereafter.

After the early Christian era, it became more and more commonplace for Christians—under cultural influences from the surrounding Greco-Roman culture—to spiritualize God and to understand God as radically distinct from matter. So the affirmation that "God is [the] spirit" tended to become the assumption that God is spiritual. Fast-forward now to our own time, when we can hear two professors of theology at a Catholic college in the US explain, in a popular manual, published by an evangelical press in 1999: "By saying God is spiritual, we mean that God is not a material being . . . God must be immaterial, that is, spiritual."

The assumption here is that God's relation to the material order of creation is primarily a matter of *pronounced distance*, and that God's own identity is *radically different* from the material world. The same kind of thinking holds that the human creature, made in the image of God, is, although embodied, likewise essentially different from material nature generally. Humans alone, after all, have immortal souls, right? Or so many Christians have been taught to believe over the ages.

This puts those Christians today, who want both to affirm classical Christian teachings and to respond to the fundamentally material crises of our times in a serious predicament: Do Christians really care about *matter*? For Christians, *does matter really matter*? Try as Christians may to respond to our global crisis, if we don't think that matter really matters, where does that leave us?

And tinkering with the spiritualizing theology that many of us have inherited won't really help that much either. However much some Christians may wish to accent stewardship of nature, for example, it's still stewardship of nature. It's still assuming that nature is some lesser thing that can be managed and should be managed, compared to the human spirit, which has value in itself. We Christians must therefore come face-to-face with this challenge: We can no longer hold on to a theology that values spirit over matter. *We need a theology which treasures matter just as much as spirit.*

Theologian Paul Tillich once published a book of sermons titled *The Shaking of the Foundations.* That's probably what we need here when we're still taking the traditional Christian teaching that "God is spirit" for granted. We need to feel the foundations shaking. We need an understanding of God that's materially richer than the traditional spiritual kind of understanding that many of us have inherited.

II.

So I'm led to this observation: Ironically perhaps, much of traditional Christian theology *has* depended fundamentally on seeing God through a *natural* lens, although not always being aware of that fact. The result has been a certain kind of spiritualizing, with this assumption: the God who is pure spirit is *like the sun.* Call this *the hierarchy of Light Inaccessible.*

This is the idea. Imagine Henry David Thoreau and his party ascending Mount Katahdin in Maine. Although Thoreau himself never thought of such an ascent as reaching out for a vision of God above nature, many Christians throughout the ages have done precisely that. They have sought to find their way to God as the One who dwells far above the earth. You climb to the top of the mountain and you look up. There God dwells in Light Inaccessible. Or so many Christians throughout the ages have been taught to believe. Gothic architecture, with its soaring heights, pointing to God above, is but one revealing instance of such convictions.

Along the way, moreover, Christians also imagined themselves climbing up to those heights spiritually through different levels of the created world on a kind of ladder: sheer matter is at the bottom, then comes formed physical matter (plants, and animals), followed by the embodied human world of matter and spirit (or body and soul); further ascent leads to and through the angelic world of pure finite spirits, and finally we stand beneath the ineffable, incomprehensible world of infinite spirit, God. From this traditional Christian perspective, God is like the sun, totally above and removed from all earthly realities, blindingly incomprehensible. God, in this sense, is *the Ineffable Above*.

This is my proposal; I'm sure that Thoreau would never have agreed, but he might have sympathized with my intent: Yes, hold on to the vision of God as the supernatural Sun, the Light of lights, *the Ineffable Above*. That tells a truth, but not the whole truth. Think also, therefore, of God as material, as well as spiritual. Think of God as *the Ineffable In, With, and Under*, not just the Ineffable Above. This is why I want to take you to Niagara Falls. Why not think of God being as much like the Niagara River and its falls as God is also like the sun?

III.

Why are we doing this? Think of the size and age of our universe, populated as it is with some five hundred billion galaxies, thirteen billion years old and still expanding. Our thoughts about God must be commensurate with a universe like this. But generally theological and spiritual reflection these days, I have observed, is much more limited. It typically has a default focus that is *geocentric* (if not totally *anthropocentric*) when nature is being discussed, as if God were chiefly the God of human life on planet Earth.

Such reflections often suppress, as well, reference to gargantuan terrestrial phenomena such as tsunamis, earthquakes, volcanic eruptions, or epidemics like COVID-19. On the contrary, the triune God, in addition to everything else, is a God of astounding torrential power, in, with, and under all the cosmic immensities, near and far—not just the God of human life, nor just the God of various placid human encounters with nature here on planet Earth.

True, the theme of divine power is in some respects problematic, particularly when it is construed abstractly in terms of God's *omnipotence*. I remember asking my sixth-grade Sunday school teacher, Mr. Popper, who was a key church figure for me in my early years, "If God is omnipotent, can he create a rock so heavy that he can't lift it?" Mr. Popper replied, "Some things we can't understand." Yes. But we *can* understand that (as Martin Luther and John Calvin were wont to say) God's power is *what God actually does, amazingly,* throughout the whole creation, from first things to last, not what God in principle could or could not do.

Furthermore, we will want to understand God's power as *real* power in this context, not as something else (perhaps some force next to nothing, as if God were just hanging around, but not doing anything). To be sure, there are undoubtedly *gradations* of Divine power, as God relates, say, to a human decision, on the one hand, using a kind of persuasive power, or to the collapse of a galaxy, on the other hand, employing a kind of colossal coercive force, beyond anything that we can possibly imagine. As Calvin was wont to suggest, God *accommodates* the use of God's power to a variety of different creatures.

Divine power, one might say, is in some respects like the sounds that a piano can produce. Sometimes the sound is a single note. Sometimes it's several notes in harmony. It may also be many sounds together, like a Beethoven sonata. On occasion, it may be a cacophony, with an effusion of notes in loud, even bombastic disharmony—as if some child were exuberantly pounding the keyboard with both fists. God accommodates Godself in the use of God's power to a variety of different creatures in a variety of different ways that take into account and respect the integrity of each creature. Still, God *does* relate to all creatures, powerfully.

The point is this. We do not want to end up with a vision of a God who is imaginably adept at inspiring humans or even influencing the birds of the air, yet who is not imaginably adept at influencing the oceans or the permutations of dark matter.

This brings me to the primary thought I want to underline here. *The triune God of Christian faith is natural as well as spiritual.* The analogy of God as spiritual should not be privileged. God must be thought of in terms of nature analogies as well as in terms of social analogies or personal analogies, necessary as these are. Unless nature is a primary analogy for God, as a matter of fact, nature—especially when it is understood cosmically (that is, in terms of the whole universe or all universes)—will essentially remain something distant from God or even alien to God.

IV.

You may not have heard anything like this from whomever might have been your Mr. Popper in Sunday school or even in sermons over the years, but this kind of thinking about God in conjunction with nature is as biblical as the day is long. The living God confessed by biblical traditions is as much akin to nature and its complexities and powers and immensities as this God is akin to human social relationships or to personal interactions.

Consider this testimony from Psalm 29: "The voice of the Lord is over the waters; the God of glory thunders, the Lord over the mighty waters. The voice of the Lord is powerful; the voice of the Lord is full of majesty . . . The Lord sits enthroned over the flood" (verses 3–4, 10) Similar images appear dramatically in the book of Job, chapters 37–40. So the Lord is presented as saying to Job, memorably:

> Where were you when I laid the foundations of the earth?
> . . .
> Or who shut in the sea with doors
>   when in burst out from the womb—
> when I made the clouds its garment
>   and thick darkness its swaddling band . . .?
> . . .

Have you entered into the springs of the sea,
     or walked in the recesses of the deep?

. . .

Who has cut a channel for the torrents of rain
     and a way for the thunderbolt,
to bring rain on a land where no one lives,
     on the desert, which is empty of human life

. . . ?

Has the rain a father,
     or who has begotten the drops of the dew?
From whose womb did the ice come forth,
     and who has given birth to the hoarfrost of heaven?

. . .

Can you lift up your voice to the clouds
     so that a flood of waters may cover you?
Can you send forth lightnings . . . ? (Job 38:4–35)

From Job to the New Testament now. I sense the same kind of primal power attested in Mark's account of the disciples on the Sea of Galilee. A storm comes upon them, and they fear for their lives. In a large painting, Rembrandt once dramatized this scene in darkly and chaotically hued oils, showing the disciples and Jesus in a small sailing vessel that is being tossed over sideways and swamped by ferocious waves. The passage from Mark suggests no less.

The Markan text then shows us Jesus, in the words of the popular song, as "the man who stilled the waters" (Mark 4:35–41). Some scholars who have studied this story have cautiously spoken of the *Divine luminosity* of Jesus taken for granted by its Markan author, befitting one who is regarded by Mark as the Son of the very God who is the Creator of all things. The storm text itself ends with this haunting question: "Who then is this, that even the wind and the sea obey him?" (Mark 4:41).

Such images of God working gloriously amid the torrents of the primeval waters and of Jesus as the Lord of those very waters have fascinated me since the earliest days of my seminary studies, doubtless because of a range of experiences of my own with water in many of its manifestations, peaceful and chaotic, particularly the Niagara River. It is to that world that I now want to take you, as I promised at the outset.

V.

As I have had occasion to observe more than once above, I grew up outside of Buffalo, New York, which is not that far from the Niagara River and it falls. Already as a young child, I was fascinated with that majestic river, as its waters seemed to propel themselves from Lake Erie toward and over the magnificent thundering of the Falls, and then through the huge and gaping Niagara River gorge on into Lake Ontario thirty-five miles away. Living as close to the Falls as my family did, we visited them often, both because they were such an astounding sight in themselves, and because friends and family members from around the country found that our home was a convenient station on *their* way to visit the Falls.

When I was in high school, in the midst of the sometimes-oppressive summer heat, my friends and I would on occasion jump into someone's car and head for the Niagara River. Our destination was only halfway between Lake Erie and the Falls, but we thought of the Falls intensely as we plunged into the surging river waters far above the Falls, to see if we could make any headway swimming upstream. We couldn't.

Obviously, we were horrified by the thought of being carried too far downstream. Images of helpless human bodies being swept along by the torrents and then over the Falls filled our minds. But it was safe enough for us, all of us accomplished swimmers, as we flailed our arms at the height of our youthful powers against the currents, only to remain stationary. In retrospect, I think that that swimming upstream from the Falls was a kind of safe adolescent dancing with death.

Who can describe Niagara Falls, this icon of the historic North American consciousness? Many writers and countless painters have tried. I will only tell what little I know. The Falls were formed at the end of the last ice age. Waters from three of the bodies now called the Great Lakes carved out these Falls, leaving the gigantic river gorge before them, as those waters made their way forward, eventually, to the Atlantic Ocean and as they relentlessly chiseled away at the bedrock underneath, inching the Falls ever closer back toward Lake Erie. Niagara Falls has moved back seven miles in some twelve thousand years and may in this respect be the fastest moving waterfalls in the world.

Today, over the two separate branches of the Falls, the American and the Canadian, more than six million cubic feet of water fall every minute during the daylight hours. They plunge over heights that reach as high as 170 feet, and they extend more than a half mile wide. Thundering is indeed a good word to describe the impression they make when you stand on the observation platform, feet away from the apex of the Falls. My brother remembers feeling the ground tremble under his feet at that point, on the Canadian side, when he stood there as a boy. Sometimes, looking down from that point, he and I would watch a little ship—it looked like a toy—far below in the gorge, often obscured by the mist (the ship was called the *Maid of the Mist*) making its way toward the Falls, with yellow-coated tourists packed precariously, it seemed to me, on its decks.

Often, when my family had visitors and we motored down to see the Falls, after we had come home I would go to bed at night astounded. I would lie there thinking to myself: never mind whether I'm awake or asleep, those tons and tons of water keep flowing over the Falls and keep carving out the gorge without ceasing! It was truly an awe-inspiring memory for me as I lay there in the solitude of my bed. To be sure, things have changed with the nightly flow of the waters over the Falls since my day; the river is now diverted at night, to produce electricity. But permit me to treasure that memory of the Falls flowing majestically all night long.

VI.

Consider now the mysterious majesty of the God whom Christians hold dear, the God of our baptism, Father, Son, and Holy Spirit. I discussed some of the challenges of talking about God in this manner, as Trinity, in Chapter 1. Here I want to explore some more substantive matters. To this end, I invite you to let your imagination run wild, akin to the river itself. Remembering that God is not only transcendentally spiritual, think with me now of our *sublimely natural God*, Father, Son, and Holy Spirit, and call to mind images from the Niagara River and its falls.

Focus on the Falls themselves to begin with, ever overflowing, we can imagine, throwing down immense cascades of water every second of the day. *God the Father is like that*, always and ever overflowing with goodness and creativity, however alien to us that goodness and creativity might sometimes be, however much it might appear to us to be destructivity. In this complex sense, God is always and ever, indeed eternally, God *the Giver*. Whether we humans sleep or not, whether we notice it or not, the Father is constantly and creatively pouring forth goodness and power, from alpha to omega, from the beginning to the ending, of the whole creation.

Notice, further, that those waters that pour over the Falls are thereafter channeled for many miles. The towering cliffs lining the river below the Falls can be understood as keeping those waters moving in a single direction rather than chaotically flooding everywhere. The cliffs offer a kind of good order to the waters below, almost the way a parent does, when he or she puts boundaries in place where the children are to play by their own inspiration, and so avoid the dangers of the chaos that might overcome them, outside those boundaries. The cliffs, as it were, channel the overflowing divine goodness and creativity in the specific direction toward the vast basin of Lake Ontario, and thus enhance the richness of that goodness and creativity.

And more. Early on in the Christian tradition, the "Word," referred to in the first chapter of John, was interpreted in the philosophical categories of the day *as the structuring power* of the whole creation—that Divine structuring that "holds all things together" (see Colossians 1:17). The eternal Son of the Father, called the Word (or the Logos) of God, was understood to be the divine agency that, as it embraces all things, gives form and good order to each creature and all creatures together, from the beginning to the ending of the created world. Thus I imagine the cliffs of the Niagara River gorge, on either side of the river below, as a *gift* in a certain sense: a gift of order and direction, even a cosmic embrace.

So we have this image thus far. The overflowing creative but incomprehensible goodness of the Father—the Giver—is akin to the waters cascading over the Falls. The shaping and directing functions of the cliffs downriver from the Falls are akin to the majestic workings of the eternal Son or Logos—the Gift—holding all things together, shaping and directing all things toward their fulfilment in the eternal Future of God, as the river flows on into the vast reaches of Lake Ontario.

But do not overlook the turbulence of the waters, especially at the base of the Falls, as they cascade down into virtually immeasurable currents and eddies and countercurrents and countereddies. Contemplate that turbulence. That apparently chaotic churning appears to be what moves those waters downstream and works to carve out ever new ways for the pulsating river to rush on toward its resting place in Lake Ontario. That turbulence, I often think, is like the work of the Spirit, the "Lifegiver" announced in the New Testament.

That turbulence, in turn, is akin to the New Testament vision of the chaotic "tongues of fire" (Acts 2:2) that fell on ordinary men and women and drove them to become saints and martyrs. It suggests to me also the impulsive life force of God that draws the evolutionary history of our cosmos forward toward its eternal resting place in God. It recalls, likewise, the image of the breath or spirit of God "hovering" creatively—giving birth is what the text suggests—over the primeval waters of the first days of creation depicted in Genesis 1.

Christian interpreters of Genesis 1 by the second century understood that "breath" or "spirit" of God to be the Spirit of the triune God, as the Gospel of John had already implied. I believe that God the Spirit is both eternally and temporally akin to that amazing and overwhelming turbulence. Hence, I like to call the Spirit the *Giving*, as the Father and the Son are the Giver and the Gift.

Sometimes, when I was a young boy and had just returned from a visit to the Falls, I would spend an inordinate amount of time in my bath just before going to bed. I would use all the force available to my boyish arms to swirl those waters in what I imagined to be a hundred different directions from one end of the tub to the other. As I did, I would contemplate all the currents and eddies, insofar as I could see them. And I would recall the turbulence of the Niagara River at the base of the Falls and beyond, and I would marvel at its complexities and its power and its mystery.

I now believe that the Spirit of God once worked on the self of that young boy as he would often stand near the Falls, as he contemplated the overflowing waters—ever flowing, it seemed, in his mind and heart—and the work of the river walls below that captured and channeled that overflowing, even as those currents were astoundingly turbulent, moving in ways that no mortal mind could predict or understand. So I thought in those days—and so I still think, as I dream dreams and see visions of God, Father, Son, and Holy Spirit, Giver, Gift, and Giving.

VII.

Get a grip on yourself, then. Isn't it in reach of most Christian eco-activists in our day to think of God not just in spiritual terms as *the ineffable Above* but also in material terms as *the ineffable In, With, and Under*? Can you not envision the triune God as the One who is resplendent with the glory of eternally overflowing creative goodness, as the One who holds and shapes all creatures for countless cosmic eons, and as the One who moves the flux of all things wondrously toward the eternal cosmic fulfilment for which they were first created?

I believe that Christian ecoactivists may be uniquely equipped to claim such a glorious and many-splendored vision of God and, at appropriate times and places, to share it with others. You know nature. You have encountered nature, many of you, in wilderness treks as well as in neighborhood gardens; as you made your way alongside cascading rivers as well as around placid park ponds; when you stood next to mighty oaks in a nearby forest as well as next to exquisite roses planted at the doors of your church sanctuary.

You may well have stood with Indigenous people, too, at one time or another, on their ancestral land, feeling the turbulent works of the Spirit everywhere as you prayed with them for that land to be kept sacrosanct. More widely, your soul almost literally aches when you think of the endangered primal forests of our planet. You may even have visited wild and sublime places like the Amazon or the Tsongas. And you groan within—with the groaning of the whole creation—when you think about what is happening all around God's good earth today, how so much in particular, in so many places, is burning or melting or flooding.

This equips you as a person of faith both to celebrate and to share this vision of our sublimely natural God, who is in some ways, as we stretch our imaginations to their limits, like the Niagara River and its falls. "Deep calls to deep," says the psalmist (Psalm 42:7). You are equipped by the Spirit to know such things, experientially. Many of you are much more than ecoactivists. You have encountered some of the mysteries and the agonies and the glories of the whole creation. You want to save the earth as we know it today, not only so that it can be a just home for humans and other earthly creatures for the foreseeable future, but also because it is an immense and variegated jewel of beauty and vitality sailing through the dark seas of cosmic history.

I encourage you to keep cultivating the faith that you've been given. You have the eyes of faith to see nature as through a glass darkly. Keep probing the mysteries of God in nature—to see what more you can see.

8

Confronting the End of Nature

Spiritual Liminality on the Big Island

Was it necessary to fly to Hawaii from Massachusetts in order to confront the End of Nature (Bill McKibben)? No. Was it necessary to do a popular tourist thing in order to approach the edges of ordinary human experience? Again, no. But that was the surprise that awaited me when Laurel and I disembarked from our plane on the Big Island—this sometime before the emergence of the COVID-19 pandemic.

In many ways this was to be a liminal pilgrimage for me—to contemplate the end of nature. The days on the Big Island kept pressing my consciousness to the limits. Many times, our journey took us to places that I felt were charged with Divinity. I want to describe some of those experiences here as best I can, in order to encourage you to be attentive, in your own way, when you're approaching the edges of your own experience, particularly when you're self-consciously encountering the world of nature.

I.

On a half-rainy day in January 2020, exploring back roads near the coast in the Hilo area of the Big Island of Hawaii, the two of us came upon an almost invisible seaside park, accessible only down a cliff by a steep drop of caged-in, circular stairs. At the water's edge, overlooking the waves that were crashing on the black volcanic rocks, was a single picnic table. Sitting there in the occasional sunshine while holding our books and reading now and again, we kept lifting up our eyes to contemplate the magnificent waves of the Pacific that were rolling in and smashing against the cliffs on either side of us.

That we both had books with us was no happenstance. We carry them with us the way many other travelers carry smartphones. We take our books with us on outings, like on that coastal adventure. Before COVID, when we were doing such things, we sometimes would take our books with us out to dinner. We regularly took them with us on the subway on the way to concerts. Except for exceptions, to this very day, we take them to bed with us at night.

Recent generations may not understand. But more often than not, Laurel and I find that our books and our conversations about them day or night, are charged with engaging, sometimes exciting discoveries. She reads mostly detective novels, and I read mainly—don't be surprised—theology books. I sometimes think, we both are engrossed in mysteries!

On occasion I'll read novels, such as the one I had in hand at that little coastal park, Richard Powers's *The Overstory*. This long and complex but illuminating and deeply troubling book claimed all my reading energies during our ten-day Big Island explorations. I was fascinated, but by no means surprised, by Powers's passion for trees. I immediately decided that I had found a soulmate. As my narratives in Chapters 2 and 3 of this book have already announced, long before I began to work my way through the Powers novel, I had been blessed with a deep love and awe for trees.

But it was only recently, thanks to a number of popular books and scholarly essays, that I have been able to grasp more about the lives of trees themselves. A typical old growth forest, it turns out, is a kind of cooperative community with many parts working together—by no means just a Darwinian struggle for existence. There is competition for sure, but there is also a certain kind of responsive interaction and even mutual support.

The narrative of *Overstory* focuses on the life of a woman who knew such things deeply and who subsequently became a leader in her field, for a long time against much opposition from her scholarly peers. And that character was inspired, as Powers himself has said, by a scholar of our own times, Suzanne Simard, who grew up in the midst of old growth forests in Canada. Simard's pioneering research showed that different species of trees share resources in the forest by their fungal root interactions.

The Powers novel also brought back memories of my own environmental activism during the last sixty years—not nearly so radical, for sure, as the protests of a number of his well-etched characters. On the other hand, if theology is radical in the sense that it's a discourse that seeks to unearth the Divine roots (*radix*) of critical cosmic and historical meanings, I've been a radical, however low-key, since the 1960s, committed at every step along the way to keep encouraging other Christians to get ecologically rerooted.

As I've already observed, I did a lot of talking about theology and ecology around the country in the '70s and '80s of the last century, particularly at church colleges and in church camp settings. Along with this, as, again, I've already noted, I was a kind of ecojustice rabble-rouser at Wellesley College during the thirteen years that I served there, beginning in 1969. Also I was able to invest in the ministry of the Boston Industrial Mission (BIM) in those days, whose board I chaired for many years. Led at that time by two nationally recognized progressive and theologically gifted Episcopal priests, Scott Paradise and Norman Faramelli, BIM made a unique contribution in ecumenical church circles in that era. BIM was committed both to justice, especially urban justice, and to ecological understanding, locally and around the globe—all from a faith perspective.

More recently, I joined a campaign to pressure my own college to divest from fossil fuels. Can one voice help? I believe so. And Laurel and I do our best to support ecojustice candidates for political office, both locally and nationally. We also try to do many of the simple lifestyle things like recycling, driving a highly efficient car, and eating low off the food chain as much as we can. We have participated in public protests, too, such as the great climate protest march in New York City in the fall of 2014. But I have always considered my own environmental activism to have been modest at best.

Truth be known, though, as we began our drive around the Big Island, in odd moments I kept thinking not so much about environmental activism but about something else. Was it a contradiction for the two of us to have contributed so blatantly to the global climate crisis by choosing *to fly* to Hawaii and back? I read not too ago that the share of carbon emissions of *one* of us on such a round trip flight from Boston to Hawaii would almost equal the amount of emissions we might have avoided had we decided to go totally car-free the whole previous year. Something about which our theological forebears knew virtually nothing had thereby reared its ugly head in my own spiritual world, and not for the first time, by any means—ecoguilt.

On the other hand, I realize that when I entertain such thoughts, I can also conveniently invoke Martin Luther's bon mot, often quoted by theological writers: "sin boldly, but trust all the more in the Lord, and rejoice." Theologically trained people like me love such thoughts. In a word, don't get hung up on your guilt! But I am also well aware of the mental gymnastics that those thoughts sometimes entail. So at some point along the way on the Big Island I decided not to worry about ecoguilt, but just to live with the contradictions and then to keep throwing myself into our travel. Was that the wisdom or the folly of old age—or perhaps both?

So it happened that early on in our journey I found myself intensely preoccupied not with ecoguilt, but with what I came to think of, with Powers's help, as the great *overstory*, and by what that story meant for me and for Laurel and for our children and our grandchildren and indeed for all the creatures of the earth, now and in generations to come. I kept thinking, *The trees! The trees! The trees!* Especially their absence! As our trip unfolded—except for the eastern shore of the Big Island, where everything would come to a conclusion for me—trees were often in evidence to us on the Big Island mainly because they were *not* to be seen. Was this a sign of things to come in other regions of the earth? Where were all the trees?

I had tried to deal with this question before we departed for Hawaii. Alas, however, I couldn't learn very much. Only this: In primordial times, plant seeds generally were very slow to arrive on the volcanic islands of Hawaii. Single seeds established themselves only rarely, once every hundred thousand years, carried in by migratory birds perchance. But when the Polynesians arrived fifteen hundred years ago, they did find a number of areas teeming with many different kinds of plants and trees.

What then had become of those green riches over the centuries? I wasn't sure. I speculated that vast areas had been destroyed by volcanic eruptions. Then there was always the possibility of devastation by humans, too, especially in modern times, say, to make way for sugar plantations. Did trees ever cover the Big Island as a canopy? From what I could learn in cursory readings, that is highly unlikely. Add to that the consistently sparse rainfall in many areas of the Big Island, at least in the modern era, and no wonder that that place appeared to me at times to be much more a vast black wasteland than anything remotely descended from some primally green garden of Eden.

II.

But I am getting ahead of myself. While the story of the great overstory—or its absence—constantly hovered in my mind, I found myself much more immediately engaged in the first days of our trip with mundanities. With the city of Hilo itself, for example. A former sugarcane outpost, Hilo seemed to me still to be very much a working-class town. Much of its coastline is replete with warehouses and loading docks and corner stores, notwithstanding the obvious efforts that had been made to spruce it up with seaside parks and upscale hotels.

At Hilo, fittingly, Laurel and I stayed for a day at a small, cheap hotel. Nearby, at a restaurant that appeared to be frequented mainly by locals, we enjoyed unusually spiced drinks before dinner, the one flavored with hibiscus, the other with jalapeño. The restaurant itself was perched on posts, in anticipation of the next tsunami. But never mind that kind of calamity, probably those posts wouldn't help all that much, I concluded, when, after its next eruption, Mauna Loa would begin to send its lava flows relentlessly down to the sea. Had I therefore in that restaurant stumbled onto a historic insight that was obvious to anyone who lived on the Big Island? Was that perhaps the story of this region of Hawaii, if not all the islands, a richly flavored human world that was constantly vulnerable to natural disasters?

The following day we left Hilo and drove for several hours along the arid northwest coast of the Big Island, many outcroppings of which were gargantuan, and some of which made up an enormous miles-wide sloping flatland of what were for us alien lava fields. Those regions appeared to us to be akin to what we knew of the surface of the moon, but astonishingly black, not grey, and pervasively jagged. They were almost totally devoid of trees too, often devoid even of grasses.

III.

Kailua-Kona, our destination on the western coast, was greener, thanks to more frequent rainfall. There we stayed at a small house, which we had all to ourselves, maybe ten yards from the thundering waves at high tide. One day we watched a wiry young man emerge from the scarcely visible house adjacent to ours, hidden by a wall of small trees. He easily balanced himself on protruding lava rocks some yards out into the turbulent tidal waters. He carried what turned out to be a sizeable white net, which he then repeatedly and gracefully cast over the waves. We wondered what he was fishing for. But, notwithstanding his elegant movements, he didn't seem to catch anything. Was that a parable for our times? No, I didn't want to read too much into that simple story. Sometimes fishing is—just fishing.

Another day, as we were reading on the back porch, overlooking the waves, we heard the sound of what seemed to be an extraordinary wave crashing onto the dark lava shoreline wall below us. On second glance, I discovered the source of that huge, resonant noise. It was a massive humpback whale, maybe a quarter mile offshore, surfacing and then crashing back into the waters. On cue, a remarkably smaller whale calf arose and crashed into the waters with much less resounding thunder. That wonderful duet then repeated itself two more times!

I felt at that moment that something of the Divine mystery of creation had just been disclosed to me, reminiscent of Job's much more comprehensive experiences at the edge of his wilderness. Although I have never been good at remembering Bible verses, as I contemplated those glorious creatures frolicking (if indeed it was frolicking), that astounding verse in Psalm 104 came to mind, about God creating the sea monsters *to play with them*—and also the verse in Psalm 145 about the Divine resolve to give them their food in due season.

At Kailu-Kona we also occupied ourselves with snorkeling, which had been the chief purpose of each of our three other Hawaiian trips over the years. Snorkeling has been Laurel's passion mainly, although I—once a competitive swimmer—have eagerly paddled along with her in every instance and in every direction. On one occasion, on an earlier trip, I lost sight of her. I was frightened.

Turns out that she had taken off on her own to swim around a little island, perhaps a hundred yards offshore. I had urged her not to do that, since I constantly carried with me a possibly deranged fear of sharks. But my desire to be with her trumped that fear, and I soon made haste to find her. I caught up with her on the other side of that little island, where no one—no lifeguard, for sure—could see us. But my dark fears, which perhaps told more about me than about the conditions of snorkeling in that area, subsided, once we had rounded the island and could see the shore again.

The word *snorkeling*, I know, sounds odd. (It's a recent word, borrowed from the German and having to do with breathing). It sounds almost as odd as we, two senior citizens, must have appeared when, on this occasion, we entered the waters at a public park, wearing gloves and masks, carrying air pipes and flippers—she holding my hand, me balance challenged, carefully proceeding baby step by baby step, until we finally were able to lower ourselves slowly into the thigh-deep waves, put on our flippers, adjust our masks and air pipes, and then easily swim out to deeper regions.

It was all worth it, however comical it might have appeared at the outset. There we maneuvered effortlessly, it felt, uplifted in body and spirit by the temperate, clear water and delighted by the sight of so many multicolored fish—we watching while they seemed casually to feed and then energetically to dart around the striking coral reefs maybe twelve feet below. It was as if we had been given a privileged vision of the fifth day of creation.

This was a powerful spiritual moment for me. It was quite *unlike* the "oceanic feeling" described by Sigmund Freud or by some mystics, the idea that such experiences drive you to *lose yourself* in the Divine, like a drop of water disappearing into a vast sea. On the contrary, I *found myself* in a fresh way at that moment, floating on the surface and contemplating those fish below: as one small creature among unimaginable numbers of others, from the nearly infinite in size to the infinitesimal, each one beloved by God in its own way, myself included.

While at Kailua-Kona too, we joined a contingent of other tourists for a day on a little ship, which took us all to a secluded bay several miles south to a national seaside protected area, where we snorkeled and contemplated the gorgeous fish there for two more timeless hours. After that, on board, all the passengers and the crew enjoyed a deliciously grilled commonplace repast. Did that mundane voyage and that simple lunch offer a kind of intense communion with the God who is in, with, and under and above, beyond, and beneath both the worlds of human and cosmic history? For me it did.

On another day at Kailua-Kona, we motored up winding roads to the top of a mountain precipice in order to find a funky cafe, where we had lunch at a window overlooking the whole coastline far below, bathed as it was at that time in the sun and punctuated by the shadows of a few ominous rainclouds. What human hands had shaped those vast sloping mountainside fields below us? I wondered; and more recently, what had it truly cost to develop the land closer to the ocean into sprawling residences for the rich and the powerful? And what species might have lived on those slopes in times gone by? Indigenous peoples perchance? Humans now long gone from that place—perhaps forcibly removed at some time? Was it possible, indeed, to hear the groaning of the whole creation in that richly developed setting?

IV.

After our stay at Kailua-Kona, we drove around the mountainous northern coast. We kept motoring higher and higher, with an ancient extinct volcano on one side and the vast shoreline extending from horizon to horizon below us. This was a region of immense grasslands, presumably cleared of trees (and perhaps of Indigenous peoples) at some time by colonizing human hands for the sake of sugarcane production maybe or to create flowing fields where cattle could graze. The vistas at that point, some three thousand feet high, were extraordinary.

We then descended along a narrowing and still more winding road two thousand feet or more to what appeared to be a small tourist town, Hawi, where we enjoyed an idiosyncratic Hawaiian lunch and, with all the other tourists, dutifully applauded two middle-aged native women who were doing what was billed as traditional dances. What might we have learned from that experience had we been able to find some time to talk with those dancers in a more secluded setting?

Returning to Hilo, we took eager refuge in an elegant three-floor shoreline hotel, perched on posts, again, in view of the next tsunami. The best snorkeling we experienced on our trip was at a nearby sandy beach, thankfully not, like many of the others, full of sharp lava rocks. The sun had just come out from behind some deeply dark clouds in time for our first plunge into those nearly transparent waters. The fish there were extraordinary, some of them with colors we had not seen before. We had entered their world, of course, and we felt privileged to have glimpsed it once again.

The following day, huddled together, carrying our single black umbrella under a steady rain, we walked along the dark shoreline behind our inn, tiptoeing on the sometimes-slippery volcanic stone flats at the edge of the ocean. At one point we caught sight of a grand sea turtle, which soon disappeared from sight under the ledge of the rocky shoreline on which we were standing. Such turtles, I understand, can stay underwater for as much as half an hour. On a previous Hawaiian trip, to Kauai, while snorkeling, we had glided over several similar massive creatures, none of which seemed to pay any attention to us.

From that seaside base in Hilo, the next day we drove thirty-five miles to Volcano National Park and explored its many contours and precipitous sites. Somehow the fog that often shrouded us that day seemed fitting. Every dark volcanic basin appeared to be charged with mystery. At the end of the day, as we sat in an upscale restaurant at the upper reaches of the volcano, we looked out the large picture windows, which were to have shown us beautiful scenic vistas, and we saw heavy grey clouds everywhere.

At that moment we might well have pondered the ambiguities and the contradictions of affluent human existence on planet Earth. By what right had we been expecting to be presented with a scenic view? Instead, we talked about the books we had been reading, and we gossiped about our children and our grandchildren, in the process relishing more delicious local cuisine.

During the meal, we had a fascinating conversation with our server, whose day job was caring for a dozen cattle. He complained about not being able to grow the vegetables he was eager to harvest because many of them rotted in the heavy rains in that region. It was also a challenge, he remarked, to keep the cattle dry, which he said he needed to do for their own sakes. For sure, he was much more in tune with the meanings of that region than tourists like us.

V.

Finally, while Laurel had her snorkeling moments to keep rejuvenating her spirits, the spiritual high point of the trip for me was our long, contemplative visit to the Hawaii Tropical Bioreserve and Garden not too far from Hilo, the city where we had begun our journey. The day we were at that park we had the place almost entirely to ourselves. It was full of an unimaginable number of small, large, and gargantuan plants, from variegated orchids and spider lilies to monkeypod and African tulip and banyan trees, topped off by immense palms. The park was bounded at its lower levels by the sea itself and the churning of the incoming waves.

A thoroughly modern human creation (opened in 1984) containing ground plants and vines and trees from middle-earth regions around the globe and doubtless also scores of indigenous animals that we never heard or saw (except for the songs of a few birds), this dramatically sloping almost forty-acre seaside garden, featuring as it did several cascading streams, was more than a park for me. Again I kept thinking about the trees! The trees! The trees! As I walked along the circuitous, well-designed paths, a few of them so steep that I had to hold on to Laurel so as not to lose my balance, and as I looked up at the canopy high above, I called to mind some of the themes of *Overstory*. For, in this place—not without the investment of much human capital—the overstory ruled everything else.

But all the more so, inveterate student of Scriptures that I have long aspired to be, I thought of that place as the garden of Eden. Laurel and I were Adam and Eve all over again, I imagined, fragile and dependent creatures who were almost totally hidden amid those astoundingly huge leafy plants and colossal trees. Laurel picked up the theme of human minisculity in her own characteristic fashion, calling to mind for us the half-dozen sizeable broad-leafed tropical plants that I have collected and care for in our own living room back in Massachusetts. She imagined herself at that moment in that fecund Hawaiian botanical garden, she said, as some kind of inch-high humanoid walking through an overwhelmingly green effervescence of gigantic houseplants.

For me, that exquisitely alive seaside temple of towering trees and intricately variegated flowers and mysterious vines and spaciously leafed undergrowth and crashing streams and the constantly incoming ocean waves on the Big Island also brought forth feelings of—deep sadness. What was the future of this Garden of Eden to be? Our trip happened to coincide with the weeks during 2020 when half of Australia, it seemed, was going up in flames.

VI.

You will not have been surprised by my sadness. Who among us did not follow the news of the vast Australian fires that year, and then the reports of California burning, without a sense of global dread? More recently, too, monstrous forest fires all over the North American West have become commonplace. In 2021, one fire in Oregon overran more than four hundred thousand acres, with temperatures so high that it created its own weather system under its own heat dome and sent clouds of smoke as far away as the East Coast.

And more, sadly, as readers of this book will know all too well. Signs of planetary disintegration are all around us these days, not just visible in colossal, rampaging forest fires. Hence many of us have nightmares about the world that our grandchildren will in all likelihood inherit if the principalities and powers of our earthly history continue to hold sway. Not to mention the particular threat of pandemics like COVID-19 or acts of desperation like mass human migrations. No wonder that this is the question that has weighed down the soul of virtually every Christian ecoactivist I have ever encountered. It is the question driving the prospect of the End of Nature. *Is there really any hope?*

I do believe that there *is* hope, but that that hope is by no means obvious. For me, that hope is not announced by the signs of these times. For me, real hope is revealed first and foremost in the praises of the faithful. It all hinges on singing up a different kind of storm, with tongues of fire from the Spirit. This leads me to the improbable theme that I will explore in my next and last chapter—doing nothing.

9

Doing Nothing

The Political Mission of the Church and the Global Ecojustice Crisis

One of my favorite sayings comes from an improbable source, the Freudian philosophical critic of the 1960s, Norman O. Brown: "Doing nothing is the supreme action." This is a perfect thought for Christian ecoactivists living in the United States in these times of global crisis. Let me tell you why.

I.

An irony of American history today, as many people are aware, is this: In recent years, the citizenry elected a president who announced as a candidate that "the swamp must be drained." He was referring, of course, to political life in Washington, DC, at the time of his candidacy. That the American electorate came back four years later and tossed out that candidate, then the president, in significant measure due to the corruption he appeared to have fostered in the nation's capital, is an irony, but that's not the particular point that I have in mind here.

The observation I want to make here is this: more than eighty-one million Americans *did something*. They voted for a new president in 2020. This current runs deep in the American character—activism. When something is wrong, Americans typically want to fix it! This is not the most original of sociological insights, to be sure. Thoughtful observers have noted this characteristic of American life since colonial times.

American church people tend to be much the same. Is it a mere happenstance that I'm writing this book as an activist for—activists? Is it a mere happenstance, likewise, that I concluded my reflections in Chapter 3 about Saint Francis with this mundane counsel: don't just sit there feeling guilty, do something? More generally, how many church conferences have I attended that have led the participants to this question at the end: Okay, now what are we going to do? Or, more particularly, what should our goals and objectives be? When I chaired the board meetings of the Boston Industrial Mission for many years, I almost always ended meetings with this agenda item: Assignments.

I still believe in assignments, especially for the powers that be in Washington, DC. Drain the swamp. Drain the swamp of policies that plaster over the boils of white racism. Drain the swamp of the habits of mind that promote self-styled revolutionaries to storm the Capitol. Drain the swamp of decadent and dangerous ideas like wholesale dependence on fossil fuels and dependence on military might. Drain the swamp of any idea that in this era of accelerating climate change we Americans can keep on doing business as usual at home or around the world. And I am totally on board with church and other lobbying and protest groups that are working diligently to bring a new day to Washington, DC, by organizing to foster Green New Deal policies and by fomenting the renewal of every urban neighborhood and forgotten farm community across the land, drawing on the energy and the vision of movements like Black Lives Matter.

II.

But consider Saint Francis again. Francis surely *did* many things, as we have seen. He reached out to the lepers outside the gates. He made a totally countercultural pilgrimage to visit the sultan in the name of peace during the violent era of the Crusades. He often preached repentance to unruly crowds in the city square.

But all the more so, he regularly *retreated* to remote places to pray. Whenever he could, too, he left the highways and byways of his world in order to attend Mass. His intent, indeed, was to participate in the Mass every day. And in what was perhaps the crowning public act of his entire ministry, he retreated to a mountain forest on Christmas Eve, as we have seen, and gathered farm animals and people from every station of life to join him in celebrating the Christ-Mass.

What was going on in Francis's mind and heart at that moment? We have no way of knowing. He left us no record, nor did his biographer, Thomas of Celano. We do know from Celano that Francis sang the Christmas Gospel text about the birth of the Savior. Was the song of Mother Mary, called the Magnificat, as we have it in the Gospel of Luke, also part of that Christ-Mass at Greccio, and if so, did Francis sing that part of that liturgy, too? Probably not, but we don't know.

Be that as it may, the vision of Mother Mary contemplating her newborn child and celebrating the Divine purposes that had there unfolded was in all likelihood not far from Francis's mind and heart that Christmas Eve in that forest. For Francis had a deep affection for the one whom he revered as the Mother of God. All the more so, he had profound affection, from the beginning of his public ministry to the end, for those whom Mother Mary celebrated, "the lowly." Consider her song, as we have it in the Gospel of Luke, chapter 1, verses 46–55:

> My soul magnifies the Lord,
>> and my spirit rejoices in God my Savior,
>> for he has looked with favor on the lowliness of his
>> servant.

Surely, from now on all generations will call me blessed;
>   for the Mighty One has done great things for me,
>   and holy is his name.
His mercy is for those who fear him
>   from generation to generation.
He has shown strength with his arm;
>   he has scattered the proud in the thoughts of their hearts.
He has brought down the powerful from their thrones,
>   and lifted up the lowly;
>   he has filled the hungry with good things,
>   and sent the rich away empty.
He has helped his servant Israel,
>   in remembrance of his mercy,
>   according to the promise he made to our ancestors,
>   to Abraham and to his descendants forever.

What the Gospel of Luke here identifies as Mother Mary's song might well have been a hymn familiar to Luke that was sung in a number of first-century Jewish-Christian communities in the Holy Land by the "Poor Ones," the *Anawim*—a word that originally was used, according to the New Testament scholar Joseph Fitzmyer, to denote the physically poor, but that in time came to be applied to people in Israel who were unfortunate, lowly, sick, downtrodden.

Travel in your mind's eye, then, and imagine yourself standing with St. Francis and the animals and with people of many stations of life that night in the woods for that Christ-Mass. Imagine that this song, which was always in Francis's heart, was also at this moment on his lips, which it could have been. And let the tonalities of the song sink into your own mind and heart. Hear these charged words in Mother Mary's lullaby, in particular: "My soul magnifies the Lord, / and my spirit rejoices in God my Savior / . . . / He has brought down the powerful from their thrones, / and lifted up those of low degree" (Luke 1:46–47, 52).

III.

I hear these words as having profound implications for how *we* in our time should understand *the political mission of the church and the ecojustice crisis*. To draw out these implications, I first want to review what can be called the received understanding of the political mission of the church in the US today. That understanding has two major expressions, sometimes claimed by two different groups within US churches, sometimes championed together.

According to the first view, *the political mission of the church is to inspire individuals to go out into the world to be good citizens*. This is the kind of maxim I was taught in my earliest years in the church, through my high school years. I didn't learn about this option from the Rev. Billy Graham, but this was how that great evangelist liked to think of the Christian life in society, when he wasn't trying to convert Americans to be witnesses for Christ: to be good citizens. This option for Christians in public life has much to commend it, as we learned anew in the wake of the 2020 election. Your vote can count.

According to the second view, *the political mission of the church is to inspire its members to go out into the world as change agents for the sake of justice*. This is how I tended to think in the era of the 1960s and '70s. Those were the days when many of us looked to public figures like the Rev. Dr. Martin Luther King Jr. to rally the whole society to address racism and other forms of injustice, among them environmental injustice. Many of us wanted to be change agents ourselves.

Likewise, for more recent events like the People's Climate March in 2014 in Manhattan, which was joined by countless Christian activists and by many others of goodwill. Likewise again for the Black Lives Matter street actions in 2020, which, on a single day (June 6), could draw out half a million people in nearly 550 places across the US. Thousands of Black and white Christian activists from many denominational traditions took to the streets to join with many other citizens who cared deeply for social justice in order to make their voices heard.

But I don't think that these two familiar ways to understand the political mission of the church—to be a good citizen and to be a change agent—are sufficient in themselves. Where are all the good citizens or all the change agents going to come from? To invoke a biblical metaphor, those are the good fruits. But where are the roots? The acts of the good citizens or the change agents don't just burst on to the scene out of thin air. They typically grow from good soil. And that good soil, from a pragmatic perspective, is the nurturing community of the church.

IV.

Which brings me back to Norman O. Brown: "Doing nothing is the supreme action." I believe that doing nothing can sometimes be the best of assignments for Christian ecoactivists. Doing nothing, in this case, means putting down roots into the good soil of the nurturing Christian community so that you can the more faithfully and the more forcefully go public in due course to produce the fruits of being a good citizen or a change agent or hopefully both. Any practiced gardener will know this much, on the basis of firsthand experience: the harvest doesn't happen immediately; there has to be a time for the growth.

Consider doing nothing, then, as the supreme Christian action. According to this option, the being of the church precedes the doing of the church. Doing nothing precedes doing something. Remember Mother Mary. For sure, she didn't go anywhere in public, say, into the streets or to the temple, in order to have some kind of a public impact. With Joseph, she retreated to a peasant's hut in order to have her baby—and she gave thanks. She sang a song of praise. She magnified the Lord. This suggests to me what might be called the *Magnificat Option* for understanding the political mission of the church. Praise the Lord in the community of the faithful before you set out to do the public works of the Lord.

With such thoughts in mind, the contemporary American Methodist theologian Stanley Hauerwas has argued that, in our times, church people should consider themselves first and foremost to be "resident aliens." The church is no longer "established," Hauerwas believes. Today's world, indeed, is thoroughly secular, indifferent if not hostile to the church and to other religious bodies as well. Therefore the church must nurture its own activists. Christian activism doesn't just happen. It must be cultivated in the good soil of the community of resident aliens.

For this reason, church people very much need the support of each other, Hauerwas affirms. The only way we're going to keep the faith alive, he holds, is if we who think of ourselves as followers of Jesus bond together and support each other and—worship together. I call this the Magnificat Option because the first thing you do as a person of faith is—to magnify the Lord. Figuring out how to follow Jesus in today's world—discipleship—that's the next step.

Which is to say, then, that the political mission of the church is first of all to be a community of resident aliens, who keep faith alive, especially through worship and spiritual practices, in a world that appears to be going to hell in every direction. This theme has provided me with my own marching orders—marching in place!—in recent decades. I recommend it strongly, but I do have a few reservations about it, which I will identify in a moment.

V.

The image of being a resident alien has much to commend it. You begin with a tangible communal identity. You stand for something as all stand together in the household of faith. Isn't it true that if you don't know who you are, if you don't have a firm faith identity, it's not going to be easy for you to care enough to get to the voting booth or to join a church lobbying group or to go out to the streets, not to speak of convincing others to come over to your way of looking at things and to join with you?

And then there's this: What happens when your first burst of enthusiasm wanes? What do you do when your impressive ecojustice commitments keep crashing into the closed doors of reality? Being part of a community of resident aliens gives you, or it can, the support system you need to establish and sustain your identity as a person of faith in a strange, even hostile world, and *then* to get going, again and again and again.

Being part of a community of resident aliens more particularly has the advantage of helping you to put first things first. As in the first of the two great commandments, from the law of Moses, which Jesus cited: "You shall love the Lord your God with all your heart, and with all your soul, and with all your mind." (Matthew 22:37) Put God first. Praise the Lord. Rest in the Lord.

Saint Francis, for one, participated in the Mass virtually every day of his postconversion life, as we have seen. He wasn't first and foremost some wandering friend of nature, although he was that. He wasn't first and foremost a public prophet of peace or a personally engaged doer of good, although he adopted those roles too. He was first and foremost a bonded participant in the primal ritual of the church. Everything, for him, depended on the Mass. Everything, for him, depended on, in effect, honoring the first of the two great commandments first, in the tangible way Saint Francis knew how to do that, by participating daily in the Mass, whenever that was humanly possible.

In my view, Christian ecoactivists in these times need the community that's bonded in worship more than ever. With concerned global citizens everywhere, we're all vulnerable to what the Finish Lutheran theologian Panu Pihkala has insightfully analyzed: what he calls ecoanxiety. In our world, we self-consciously live every day with dark visions of pollution and plunder of natural wealth and horrendous forest fires and gigantic floods and vast ecopoverty and, above all, an impending climate catastrophe—not to speak of the ancient enemies of human life such as tyranny or war, tsunamis or earthquakes, or plagues like COVID-19. So much of the world we live in seems so out of control so much of the time! So it's very easy, indeed, to get depressed.

Hence we need each other for moral support more than ever. And more than moral support, for sure. We need the hope that vital Christian communities can offer us. Yes, the crises before us can be depressing—sometimes even to the point of clinical depression. But together we Christians are "prisoners of hope."

(Zechariah 9:12) And we do the calisthenics of hope every time we gather for worship.

In worship we celebrate what God has already done for the world, what God is now doing for the world, and what God has promised to do for the world. We also dream utterly implausible dreams the way first-century Christians did, as they joined with Mother Mary to celebrate the arrival of the Savior and the salvation of those of low degree, like the *Anawim*.

Worship further gives us occasion to broadcast to each other the utterly implausible promises that that Savior himself brought to his people in his inaugural sermon: "The Spirit of the Lord is upon me, / because he has anointed me / to bring good news to the poor. / He has sent me to proclaim release to the captives / and recovery of sight to the blind, / to let the oppressed go free." (Luke 4:18) We worship a Savior who's not there just for us, but for everyone, especially those of low degree, wherever they may be. And we need to sing that truth together, for the sake of each one of us, so that we can then the more wisely and more creatively and more effectively *do* the truth (see James 1:22).

Worship finally gives us occasion to sing amazing praises of this Savior as the Lord of all things, with the hymnody of our first-century brothers and sisters in Colossae, as they claimed the Savior not only for themselves, not only for all peoples, not only for the earth itself, but for *the whole cosmos*: "He himself is before all things, and in him all things hold together . . . For in him all the fullness of God was pleased to dwell and through him God was pleased to reconcile to himself all things, whether on earth or in heaven, by making peace through the blood of his cross" (Colossians 1:17, 19–20). That was their cosmic hymn, sung in a time when, in their experience, all things were falling apart. That was how they testified to the conviction expressed more succinctly by the Gospel of John—"For God so loved the cosmos . . ." (3:16, my translation).

March in place and sing with your siblings in Christ, therefore, or get down on your knees or take a walk in the woods— wherever you can a find a time or place to pray. But first and foremost: *do nothing*, as the world counts such things. Praise—and pray. Because the Bible tells us so: "Sing to the LORD a new song" (Psalm 96:1) and "Be still and know that I am God" (Psalm 46:10). God has entered the world in the Child Jesus as the world's—the cosmos's—Suffering, Nonviolent Liberator. So glorify God with everything you have—heart and voice, soul and body!

True, not every Christian congregation in the US today is overflowing with inspired praises that are filled with vibrant hopes for the poor and indeed for the whole cosmos. Some Christian congregations, indeed, just seem to be going through the motions. Perhaps they can be aptly described as Winston Churchill once described the Anglican Church of his time—as "the Tory party at Prayer." More than a few members of your own congregation may not really have grasped how to lift up their hearts to glorify the Lord—body, mind, and spirit—for everything that God has done, is doing, and will do. Nor might they have developed much of a political-mission consciousness. What do you do, then, if on Sundays you feel as if you're just another member of the Tory Party at prayer?

You do one of two things: Either you can work within a vital cell of other ecojustice enthusiasts and fellow travelers in the faith, whom you can identify in your current congregation, and then together do what you can do to reform your congregation's worship and, probably, its discipleship practices, as well. Or you can find a community of resident aliens elsewhere. Pray about it. Talk with trusted Christian friends about it. And then decide where you think God wants you to worship and to serve.

And feel free to do so with a sense of urgency. For, we live in times not unlike those of the earliest Christians: *we can imagine the end of the world.* The times of humane living for the human species on earth could be much shorter than what we typically have come to take for granted. Turning things over to your current congregation's long-range planning committee might not be the best strategy. So decide as soon as you can where you belong: identify a community where you can wholeheartedly praise the Lord and learn to be an energetic disciple of the Lord, if you haven't found such a community already.

VI.

Once you've learned how to do nothing this way, by praising the Lord with your Sunday community, you'll discover that it's also possible *to do nothing in many other ways.* It *can* happen.

Catch your breath. The Lord's in charge. Not to worry. For a time, never mind rushing off to join a local protest against a pipeline project. For a time, never mind spending hours trying to figure out how to pressure your representatives in Washington DC. For a time, never mind worrying about the planning meeting you have to chair to raise funds for a protest trip to the nation's capital. For a time, never mind working half the night on your group's next mailing. For a time, never mind scheduling meetings with your own pastor to enlist support for planning a celebration of Saint Francis the first week in October. For a time, never mind trying to persuade your vestry or your church council or your congregation's board of trustees to vote to become a green congregation.

Rather, feel free to find an hour in your day or a day in your week or a season in your year just to do nothing. Then do nothing, enthusiastically. Take a walk in the woods. Hug a tree. Cultivate your vegetable garden. Go swimming in the Niagara River, safely. Walk over to the park with your dog or let your dog walk you. Contemplate the willow leaves reflected in the waters of that nearby pond. Water your houseplants. Stop and contemplate the goldfinches at your bird feeder. Sit on a park bench and watch the sun go down. Revisit the swimming hole with some old friends. Go to your hideaway and read the collected works of John Muir (!). Go snorkeling. Go canoeing. Contact a monastery near you and see what kind of retreats it sponsors; one of them might be just what you need, the world of COVID to the contrary notwithstanding. Do some cross-country skiing. Make snow angels in your front yard with some neighborhood kids. See if you can use your old ice skates somewhere. Revisit your journal. Read Psalm 104 out loud.

Write a poem about the Tsongas. Go online and visit an image of Rembrandt's painting of Jesus and the disciples on the chaotic waters of the Sea of Galilee.

Then there's your life with your immediate family, if the Lord has called you to the vocation of family living. Being in a covenanted lifelong relationship with another or participating in the dynamics of a larger household will as a matter of course rightly claim both your heart and your time, especially your time off. I imagine, for example, that Mother Mary, having magnified the Lord, might well have nursed her baby and then handed him to Joseph to care for so that she could sleep. I imagine that in due course Joseph welcomed the gesture of a nameless child in that odoriferous hovel to prepare fresh straw in the manger near the animals, so that once Mary had nursed the infant again, she could lay him there. Doing nothing in this family way, if that's where you find yourself, is surely also a supreme action.

You can do nothing from time to time during the week in many ways like these, and do so enthusiastically, because your faith and your hope and your love are built on this firm foundation: that the God whom you worship on Sundays is always near, in, with, and under all things, and this God will always be faithful and will always keep working to keep the Divine promises of salvation for all creatures at all times and in all places—including you, in the place where you find yourself. Above all, remember, *God* is going to save the world; you don't have to.

Roland Bainton, the great Reformation scholar from the last century, once told this story about Martin Luther. The Reformer apparently had just finished preaching a passionate sermon on the moral responsibilities of all Christians, in response to the free grace of God. As was his wont, Luther thereafter retired with some friends to the nearest pub. In due course, one of Luther's most zealous followers ran up to him and said something like this: "Dr. Luther, Dr. Luther, after you have just preached such a rousing sermon, challenging us to do so much, how can you just sit there?" Luther reportedly responded, "As I drink my Wittenberg beer, the gospel runs its course."

Apocryphal or not, that statement tells a certain truth. There's a time in the life of faith to drink your Wittenberg beer; a time to revel in the blessings of God; a time to sing the Magnificat joyfully with Mother Mary; a time, in that sense, to recall Norman O. Brown's words, to do nothing, as the world counts such things, for that then is the supreme action.

VII.

Of course there's also a time and place for discipleship. And this is my critical note regarding the third political mission option that I am now commending to you—doing nothing as you magnify the Lord. The reason for this critical note is this: Current advocates of this Magnificat Option (although perhaps not Stanley Hauwerwas himself) all too often have tended to suggest *not* that doing nothing is the *supreme* option, but that doing nothing is the *only* option.

They all too often seem to presuppose that the times in which we are living are so decadent and so hostile to the faith of the church that the best thing for us Christians to do is to wall ourselves off from a corrupt world and to conserve the spiritual energies we have, as some Christian monks appear to have tried to do in the early Middle Ages. This is called by some "the Benedict Option" (with questionable historical justification), which is alleged to have been the vision of one of the founding fathers of Western monasticism for our own times. In a word, build a wall around the church and pray for the best.

On the contrary, the church of Christ—and of his follower Saint Francis—has no walls without doors (I could tell a similar story, in a different way, about Saint Benedict and many of the monasteries that took his name). This church's physical sanctuary, indeed, is replete with open doors all around the building. This is because once this church has paused to magnify the Lord, it's always *a church with an itinerary*. Like the Good Samaritan, its members proceed along the roads of this world and earnestly serve the creatures in need whom they encounter there. In this sense, the Magnificat Option for understanding the political mission of the church is this: *Do nothing, for that is the supreme action—but then get going.*

That's what happened, surely, when Saint Francis's Christ-Mass in the forest had to come to an end. Somebody had to lead the animals back to their evening enclosures. Somebody had to carry the sleeping children home. Somebody had to take the Cup back to its cupboard. Others had to guide those like the elderly or people with disabilities through the forest darkness back to some kind of safe haven. Everyone had to find a way home, with help or not, because it would soon be a new day.

When I was in southern Africa in 1985 at the height of the apartheid crisis, after the Sunday liturgies had concluded in the Black churches where our delegation of visitors had worshiped, the people sometimes would exit the church building, with us in tow, singing the Zulu hymn "Siyahamba" ("We Are Marching in the Light of God"). Sometimes they would dance in a circle in front of the church building, with "Siyahamba" still on their lips. We Americans typically stood there, amazed, and applauding. Then they would be on their way along the streets of this world, many doubtless humming that same hymn—as we certainly kept that hymn in our hearts and, often, on our lips.

Now the time has come, at the end of this book, for me to invite every Christian ecoactivist to consider taking these words to heart. Yes, doing nothing is the supreme action. But a new day is about to dawn.

For God so loved the cosmos! The love of God has taken on flesh in Jesus Christ. He, the Suffering, Nonviolent Liberator of this world, born of Mother Mary, is beckoning us now to join his primal ministry to the *Anawim*. And the Spirit who drove the Poverello to follow that Liberator into the fields and the mountains and the city squares, loving every creature along the way, especially the lowly, has been unleashed once again, to empower us all to minister "to the least of these" (see Matthew 25:40).

Therefore, having claimed the Magnificat Option as your own, go preach to the birds. Go teach about the lilies of the fields. Go minister to the lepers. Go march nonviolently on Washington,

DC. Go reach out to the poor, wherever they might be. Go picket in behalf of the Tsongas. Go join a delegation that's heading to support Indigenous peoples in protesting yet another pipeline. Go help to rally other graduates of your college to join in protests to call upon your college's board of trustees to divest its fossil fuel investments without delay.

And if you can, as I very much hope that you will be able to do, *strategize and organize*, in the Spirit. Breathe with (*con-spire*) other Christian ecoactivists and fellow travelers to change or even to transform those institutions of our world that have been so corrupted by the powers of this world. Plunge head over heels into the conspiratorial ministry of Jesus Christ to the whole world.

Be a good citizen, however you can. Be a faithful change agent, in the most effective way you can. Be both if you possibly can. Organize, for sure, whenever you can. The time to get going again has arrived.

Other Books by the Author

Brother Earth: Nature, God, and Ecology in a Time of Crisis. New York: Nelson, 1970.

The Travail of Nature: The Ambiguous Ecological Promise of Christian Theology. Philadelphia: Fortress, 1985.

South African Testament: From Personal Encounter to Theological Challenge. Grand Rapids: Eerdmans, 1987.

Nature Reborn: The Ecological and Cosmic Promise of Christian Theology. Theology and the Sciences. Minneapolis: Fortress, 2000.

Ritualizing Nature: Renewing Christian Liturgy in a Time of Crisis. Minneapolis: Fortress, 2008.

Before Nature: A Christian Spirituality. Minneapolis: Fortress, 2014.

Behold the Lilies: Jesus and the Contemplation of Nature—A Primer. Eugene, OR: Cascade Books, 2017.

Celebrating Nature by Faith: Studies in Reformation Theology in an Era of Global Emergency. Eugene, OR: Cascade Books, 2020.